Hey, sometimes I don't
feel like praying

Daniel, thank you for showing me a life of prayer.
Without you, this project would not exist.

CONTENTS

We can easily spend every
waking hour focused on this
world instead of eternity to come.

FOREWORD

The wind was blowing as I stared at the tree tops from my favorite spot in the house—the back porch, with cracked wood and a few years past needing a good bucket of stain. I sat in one of those high-end plastic chairs you can buy at Home Depot for $17.99. The back of the chair leaned back, so naturally, my eyes went up with it. *How can the tops of these trees move so violently?* I thought. I have lived in this house for over five years and never once had I slowed down enough to look up at the trees. My eyes slowly tracked all the way down the tree until I realized the answer. The roots were why. The roots were the reason that on warm, snowy, windy, or even stormy days, these trees stayed right where they were planted.

Having grown up in the church my whole life, I couldn't help but begin to think about the faith and my own spiritual journey. In my mid 20s, I had lived long enough to know that life was uncertain and often full of storms. In some seasons, I felt that the things coming against me didn't affect me as much as others. In those moments, I had the realization that my roots were deep into the ground with Jesus. At other times, I would fall flat on my face, weak and helpless, by smaller issues.

I started to wonder why more followers of Jesus struggle to stay planted when uncertainties in life come. I thought back on seasons of life when I stopped going to church to pursue my own way. Why was it so easy to disconnect with God and my Christian community? Was my personal time with Him as rich and intimate as I thought it was?

Our relationship with Jesus is the true foundation of our root system. But on my back porch that day, I was looking for a more practical answer. There were two places that my mind quickly turned to: the Word of God, and our time talking to Him. I have read the Scriptures and many books surrounding topics from the Bible. I realized that what was lacking in many Christians lives (including my own) was consistency in prayer with God.

What would it look like to teach God's people to pray? This was the question I asked on that breezy afternoon on my back porch.

After getting over myself and realizing I'd never solve the problem on my own, I decided to write this little book as my contribution. It is not a 300-page theological work that will be respected for centuries, for I am no theologian. It is not a well-thought-out commentary of all of the scriptures on prayer, because that already exists.

I am writing this book not because I was good at praying but because I sucked at it. I sought for a practical solution to my inconsistency in prayer.

After being a Christian for over a decade, I prayed when I felt like it but never when I didn't. Even when I talked to God, I at times wondered why I was even doing it. I began to have a deep longing to understand prayer in the most practical of ways. I believe that prayer and walking with Jesus are *simple*. He didn't set out to confuse us or hide foundational Christian truths behind religious walls.

The more I dug into prayer, I realized this project was for single parents, third-shift workers, waitresses, college students, designers, retired grandparents, and anyone in between.

I am a follower of Jesus, a creative thinker, a business owner. I am not a pastor, priest, or theologian. This little book on prayer is simply *for the rest of us.*

I was ready to respond, but no one asked for help. I was ready to be found, but no one was looking for me. I said, 'Here I am, here I am!' to a nation that did not call on my name.

Isaiah 65:1

The moments when you want to pray the least are when you need to pray the most

INTRODUCTION

Soon after school ended, I was in a relationship, had grown a successful business, and just purchased my first home. And let's not forget the new puppy I was attempting to potty train. I had pursued and attained everything that you're told to do after school. My parents were proud of me, my followers approved of me, and my bank account supported me. Everything was running like a fine-tuned machine.

Isn't it nice when everything's going right at the start of the movie? Like most good storylines, you quickly find out that everything isn't so great. I was the only one who knew I was spiritually on life support. Everything about my life looked shiny and pretty, but the inside was rotten. I was drinking most nights, watching porn every week, and spending hours a day on social media. I had unknowingly enthroned myself as the supreme king and idol of my existence.

I was fully committed and involved in church and organized religion just a few years earlier. I would have told you I truly loved God, among all the other things. I served on leadership teams, was a volunteer staff member, and even preached a few sermons. Oh, how the prideful had fallen. I was so far from where I was just a short time before.

The God who I had spent the first part of my life knowing now felt distant. His distance was not because He left me, but because I left Him. I believed Scripture, but too many things about my life didn't add up. I had all but filed the divorce papers and sent them up to heaven.

Every external decision in my life pointed to the fact that I no longer knew nor needed a God in my life. I love in the movies when the limo driver slowly raises the shield between him and his passengers. It's always epic, and I'm sure the privacy is lovely. During this time of pursuing my own way, my prayer life with God was a lot like the limo driver. I had now raised the privacy shield and refused to look in the rear-view mirror. *God, I know You're real, and I love You, but I've got this myself.*

Most of us believe that this "God thing" is real, but there are certain areas that we'll just take care of ourselves. God, I trust You with my finances, but I can take care of my kids. I know You're the provider, but I need to handle my career on my own. The current climate teaches us to hold onto everything tightly and strive to make life work for us. The more I tried this, the more miserable I became.

I was happily dating for the first time in a year, but things took a turn. Neither of us was happy and it was evident that it might be best for us to go different directions. To be honest, they were handling this reality a bit better than me. I had become weak, dependent, and almost unwilling to speak for myself—a far cry from the guy who boldly preached on a platform to hundreds of people. I knew it was over, but I didn't have the strength to leave. I will never forget lying on my kitchen floor all by myself. I had a wine bottle beside me and I screamed out as loud as I could, "*I can't do this anymore!*"

It was at this point, at the end of my self-centered plans, that I rolled down that invisible window. I didn't look, or even speak. I just nervously and subtly made the first move. I uttered a few words lightly, but God took them seriously.

I prayed for the first time in a few years. I looked up to God and said, "Would You allow the person I'm dating to move on, because I don't have the strength to leave." Only a person desperate and borderline ill would pray such a strange prayer.

Life went on and I honestly forgot I prayed this. I woke up one day to find out they were no longer happy in our relationship. To be honest, I was mad. I screamed, cussed, and about had a mental breakdown. One night I even threw my phone and made a hole in the wall. Do you need any more proof that I was mentally unstable and spiritually on life support? Why was I having the meltdown of the century? The person I was dating was moving on.

No. *I was pitching a fit because the God I looked to had answered my prayer.*

He made it easier for me to leave because it was time. This is the time in most of our lives when we want to play the blame game. I'm unhappy and spiritually unhealthy because _____. I had to slowly begin to creep around and look in the mirror. Where I ended up was a result of my own actions and no one else's. I had let down the boundaries, ignored God, and closed down my spiritual life for the night. I had put too much on the person I was dating and I had become dependent and clingy. I wouldn't have liked myself either.

As I talked about this season of struggle with people close to me, I wanted to blame everyone. I wanted to share every angle except for the one in which I was to blame. *Until I was the center of the story I was telling myself, I would never heal.*

The relationship came to an end and it was the first domino to fall. The first hit punctured the surface and the pretty shell of my self began to crack. It wasn't long before everything in my picture-perfect (Instagram) life started to fall. I had to consciously look at why I needed a drink every night. What hole in my heart was I trying to fill by watching porn? Why did I search for significance and attention with so many hours on social media? My successful business may have been padding my pockets, but my soul had nowhere to turn. I had done what we all do: finish or leave school and begin to go after our dreams.

What I had pursued was no longer what I wanted and I was unwilling to admit it. Sometimes we'd rather stay on the wrong path that we know is destructive than turn around and admit we're wrong. I had dug a really big hole and I wasn't going to get out on my own. Someone once said that salvation is through Jesus but healing often happens in community. I had ever so kindly pushed every bit of my community away.

Why would a God who I had been ignoring for years so swiftly and kindly answer my prayer? Why would He be willing to temporarily bruise me to get me off a self-centered path that was going to wreck everything?

His answering my prayers had nothing to do with my current behavior. His response had everything to do with the fact that at 13 years old, I started a personal relationship with Him. If you've ever read Scripture, you'll know how often the writers use sheep as an analogy. Sheep may be pretty and even produce nice products, but they're dumb. Sheep make comfortable clothes, but you wouldn't want them leading you anywhere. I felt, at that moment in my life, that I was an injured sheep. Somehow I had become the one that ran away. I was anxiously, and against my will, being rescued from the thorny bush I was tangled in. It was in that moment, at the most unlikely of turns, that I learned to hear and rely on the Shepard's voice. Not only that, but I began to believe He was actually listening to mine.

In a world where we're all competing for attention, the deepest parts of our soul just want to be heard and understood. There I was, starting on the path of believing in prayer with God. I wasn't very good at it, but it was all I had.

You may look at me now, writing Christian books, serving at my church, posting YouTube videos, and think that I'm so "spiritual"— that I'm such a good person and that's why God's hand is on me. Can I argue that it's the opposite?

It's important that we establish this as we walk together on this journey of talking with God. Yes, God has blessed me and I would never deny it. But it was the terrible things about myself that actually pushed me to Him. It was the things that I hated about myself that caused me to need His love.

Why can't I stop watching porn? Why do I feel anxious all the time?

Why do I crave attention on social media? It was the things that I didn't know what to do with in the natural that forced me to face the spiritual and emotional side of my life. People wanted to think I was good and holy all of a sudden. "If only I could pray or read as much as Jordan." To be honest, it was less spiritual and more survival. It wasn't my goodness that led me toward the narrow road less traveled.

I know we are all at different places, but if there's even an ounce of you that believes the circumstances in your life, or things you've been through, somehow change how God answers your prayers, that is simply not the case. We know the devil is lying if he's talking. He is the twister and manipulator of all good things. Prayer and talking to God are really good things. If you are a child of God, the only words spoken of you are pure and good. You have nothing but a hope and a future. You are safe and secure not because of your goodness but because of His! You are more than enough, the perfect candidate for a new and improved prayer life with God.

I must warn you that as you walk down this path of discovering God, many things around and in you are going to fight so it doesn't happen. The natural often resists the supernatural. I'm sure the opposing football team would love nothing more than to cut out the communication system between the players and coaches. The devil doesn't want you linking up with the one who makes all things right. Nice analogy, you may think, but I'm not a professional athlete and I'm definitely not a five-star Christian. If you were submitting your application, you wouldn't have the degrees or the experience. I would place myself in the same category! I didn't go to seminary, so why am I qualified to write a book?

God has a consistent track record of doing things through the most unlikely of people. Scripture references multiple times that it's the uneducated, under-qualified, and humble who may see His hand at work the most. Whether we are willing to admit it or not, we all have a reason we believe that we can't easily talk to God; it could be a mistake, or even a limiting mindset about oneself.

"I'm too busy."

"I can't stay focused."

"If you only knew what I did."

"Wait, am I doing this right?"

We all have a reason, but the good news is, each one is covered. God responds to all of our concerns, precisely and simply. "Then Jesus said, 'Come to me, *all* of you who are weary and carry heavy burdens, and I will give you rest" (Matthew 11:28). If you are included in "all," then you have found the path of rest for your weary and heavy heart. "Come to me, *all* . . . who are weary."

As much as I hope you buy this book for your friends or family members, I want you for the remainder of this book to only think of one person. This was written for *you*, not for your congregation, family, spouse, or coworkers. We spend so much time doing things for God that we forget that sometimes He focuses in on us. He graciously gives us time and a space to be alone with Him. The practice of prayer is simply about talking to God. Here is the simple truth: without developing a new way to pray, I would not have made it through the season I was in. Without the hope and light of God shining in, I could clearly see how people could take their own life.

Time with God was the light shining into the darkness of my existence. Whether you are trying to get somewhere new or leave something old behind, starting or improving your prayer life has the potential to change everything.

There are so many things in our culture pulling and prying for our time and attention. You may be overwhelmed by the voices of doubt without even leaving your own head. Prayer is choosing to tie your life to the right voice. God simply waits at the door and knocks. I believe that if you're holding this book, you want to grow. I'm going to do everything I can to help that happen.

"Look! I stand at the door and knock. If you hear my voice and open the door, I will come in, and we will share a meal together as friends."

Revelation 3:20

"I pray because I can't help myself. I pray because I'm helpless. I pray because the need flows out of me all the time, waking and sleeping. It doesn't change God. It changes me."

—C. S. Lewis

You are MORE than ENOUGH, the perfect candidate for a new and improved prayer life with God.

I. FIRST

If you want to know what started me on this project, it's because my prayer life wasn't just bad, it was off the rails—filled with inconsistency, doubt, and frustration. Once a month I'd be on the living room floor, praying, crying, and surrendered in worship, but most times I'd go days or a week without a single prayer. I definitely had my "mountain top" moments with God as a believer, those experiences you dream about and don't exactly know where to store away in your memory. The inconsistency often led to either an amazing time with God or a frustrating letdown.

I want to note that I genuinely did love and serve God during this time. I did feel encouraged in community, in the Word, and in listening to sermons. The struggle was that my personal time with God wasn't quite right. It would happen when I wanted it to but never when I didn't. I would consult my earthly body on how it felt before deciding what my commitment level was to today's time with God. I would wait for that "feeling" to jump on and ride, and if I didn't feel it, I didn't do it. Other times, I would wait entirely on God and see if He would give me some momentum.

I can't say why or that I even planned this, but I started to write down little prayers in my journal. There was a quiet spot on my back porch, where the trees were blowing and the birds were chirping. I would sit down with my mind feeling so cluttered and overwhelmed. This was in a season of running a business and trying my best to provide for myself. When I would sit down, my mind was definitely not on prayer or the things of God. It was easier to think about the bills I needed to pay or the friendship that wasn't quite right.

I found that writing my prayers was a way to focus myself in the moment. I used to complain that I had a terrible memory and then I realized it was because I didn't write anything down. It was that day that I started to write down my daily thoughts. My journal became a pathway to a beautiful place with Him. I would go back to that journal most mornings and read the prayers again out loud. If I'm honest, I felt like a fraud. What kind of person has to read the same prayers every morning out loud? I was wrestling even more deeply than ever over the things I didn't understand about myself. Why did I believe the voices of doubt in my head? Why was I struggling with singleness? Why was I filled with pride and judgment toward others? Most important of all, how did all of these things affect my relationship with God?

I had found this new place of peace and serenity with Him, so why did I go back to those websites and social media apps that never satisfied? No matter your age, social class, race, or sexual orientation, obstacles in the journey of faith are inevitable. There will always seem to be something in between our place of true intimacy with God. The fact that I struggled with these things most of my life wasn't keeping me from God; I had just convinced myself it was. I still fall into mindlessly scrolling social media, but not nearly as often as I used to. I may have moments of doubt, but then I return to faith.

God was so graciously giving me time to fall in love with Him. He knew that I had been a slave to these other titles, actions, and addictions for too long. He was aware of my endless pursuit of more money and possessions. He could clearly see the things and people that I had unintentionally made into idols.

It was the infatuation of my new love that caused me to, over time, lay down the lesser. Yes, I know it didn't take you long to think of that thing in your life—the thing that you can't wrap your head around or put in a pretty little religious box. You love Jesus but you sometimes still love things that aren't best for you.

One morning after I had watched porn the night before, I opened my eyes and the first thing I remembered was "For what can separate us from the love of God?"

My goodness that makes me want to run a lap in my old Pentecostal church. I might even toss my wig or a baby. Those things you can't understand? They were never meant to fit in the box. As you spend time with God, I believe you will begin to see this truth with your own eyes. You'll still see your problem, but you'll begin in a new way to also see your God.

Temptations are not just crazy, life-altering decisions; sometimes they are small. You may not watch porn, but you could be filled with pride. You may not struggle with your identity, but maybe you're busy with no boundaries.

We are tempted every day to focus on the things that aren't right. We can easily spend every waking hour focused on this world instead of eternity to come. Thankfully we have the opportunity to look to Jesus, and when we do this we most naturally begin to pray.

Each day as I sat down to read my journal, I began to realize that I was changing, and it was happening fast. I still felt frustration at times, but I had reached another level in my personal time with God. I noticed something interesting: a consistent prayer life is better than a perfect one. God's promise that "prayer works" doesn't just apply to spontaneous moments in His presence.

God never said that prayer works only when you feel it and the song hits right. I know much of this book needs to be interpreted based on your upbringing. You could have been raised Lutheran; reading and focusing on prayer may come more naturally to you. To the Charismatic, we're often looking for the next thundering cloud of God's voice and missing the book full of His words. To the Baptist, we sway, clap, and maybe even raise a half hand when "Jesus Paid It All" hits the bridge.

If you're someone who grew up outside the church, you may not even know where to start.

I can't write this book to cover every experience you've had, but I do know one thing for sure: we all struggle with fear, insecurity, and doubt. We have at some point wondered why we need to pray and if we're even doing it right. The good news is that when we call on Him, He promises to hear our prayer and respond.

I was recently sitting by the fire with a close friend of mine. He's a worship leader and serves in full-time ministry. He was struggling with a daily time with God as we all do in the busyness of life. He said, "What do you think is one of the secrets to consistency with God?" Without even thinking I said, "I would rather spend ten minutes a day with God than to have five hours with Him once a week."

This concept is hard for us to grasp because in our current culture, more equals more. Of course you may learn and change more in five hours with God than in 70 minutes. I argue that this is not always the case. Why? Consistency creates hunger, for more of God, even if it starts small. A consistent time with God gives Him the open door to affect you in the everyday. Sure, you may learn more in that five hours once a week, but the rest of the week you've closed the door to His peace, power, and understanding.

Do you know why people addicted to porn, alcohol, or drugs have a harder time resisting than those who have never had it? It's almost impossible to have a craving for something you've never tasted. If someone says these things don't satisfy you in any way, they're lying. Many things meet a need in people's lives or else they wouldn't keep coming back to it. You often return to the feeding trough not because you're bad but because you're hungry. Porn may have been a huge part of my story, but we can even talk about social media. We all have thought, *Why do I spend so much time on this?* The more you scroll, the more you want to scroll. Social media is satisfying parts of our need to belong, to be seen and heard.

To take it a step further, these apps were designed to meet the very needs God promises to fill. These things make us feel significant, at least for a moment. They help us momentarily escape our anxiety, depression, and insecurity. The enemy would love nothing more than for us to settle for scraps as long as we don't make our way to the feast.

The devil is a professional at twisting what God created. He plays off our deepest desires to be significant, to be known and loved. He knows what our human nature craves, and he aims to take advantage when we're running on empty.

If our behavior-based struggles are caused by hunger, then we must now focus on staying filled. We will never be able to outrun our bad appetites. We have to sit down and begin to eat something new.

> "Stay alert! Watch out for your great enemy, the devil. He prowls around like a roaring lion, looking for someone to devour." (1 Peter 5:8)

When a habit slowly becomes a part of your appetite, it will naturally begin to flow into the everyday. You never used to crave a drink on the way home from work. You didn't use to worry about your spouse or kid so much. You didn't use to fight away so many lustful thoughts. The habit that you gave life to became a part of your taste.

When you begin to take ten minutes of your Netflix time to open your journal, you begin to weigh your satisfaction. Did that ten minutes with God change more than ten more minutes of TV? I can shake you and yell at you to tell you how much prayer can change your life and circumstances. I can beg you to pray for contentment, joy, and peace in your life. But until you're willing to shift a bit of your time, you'll never see for yourself.

I'm not saying to become a monk or to throw the TV off the

second-story balcony. Begin to allocate more and more of your time to the things of God. Begin to pursue the fruits of the spirit: love, joy, peace, patience, kindness, goodness, gentleness, and self-control.

Part of us believes we can't make it without social media, substance abuse, or toxic relationships. Have we paused to consider how much we're giving to these things and how often they only take from us? They promise to satisfy but leave us lacking and empty.

You must begin to take from the things that are taking from you. It's too overwhelming to think about deleting social media, unplugging Netflix, and canceling your hangouts to only pray. I am not and would not ask you to do that. I am simply challenging you to reallocate some of your time to see if the thing promising to satisfy in fact does. Jesus said something similar to a Samaritan woman who He met at the well: "Anyone who drinks this water will soon become thirsty again. But those who drink the water I give will never be thirsty again. It becomes a fresh, bubbling spring within them, giving them eternal life" (John 4:13-14).

Jesus met the Samaritan woman in the middle of her daily routine to get water and offered her something better. She responded, "Give me this water! Then I'll never be thirsty again, and I won't have to come here to get water." Her faith responded to His offer. Not only would she drink of something new, but it would satisfy her enough to leave the old things behind. For so long she had to hide in shame because of her history. With Christ, she could run and tell a whole village her story.

When it comes to your time with Him, stop focusing on the amount of time or how you feel in the moment. Simply surrender to the process and commit to doing it each day. Consistency gives God an open door into each day, an opportunity to not just be present but to bring about the help and change our souls are longing for.

I want to lead you through a series of collections that will break mindsets that we have about our need for a healthy prayer life. I will answer some questions that we're too afraid to ask—starting with why we rarely actually feel like praying.

"So let's not get tired of doing what is good. At just the right time we will reap a harvest of blessing if we don't give up."

Galatians 6:9

**A consistent prayer life is better
than a perfect one.**

We can easily spend every
waking hour focused on this
world instead of eternity to come.

II. FEELINGS

Unhealthy feelings are the greatest enemy to our place of solitude. I guess that's a mic drop, but I don't have a mic, so I'll drop my pen. Special thanks to the Holy Spirit for that one; it got me before it got you.

Sure, I'll go sit alone, read, and pray when I feel it. When I wake up and don't, it's a whole different battle. Before my prayer journal, on the mornings I wasn't feeling it, I would simply not pray. It's often hard to face the reality: I am a Christian, I love Jesus, and I don't feel like doing the thing He's asked me to do—pray. Now that I had my prayer journal, I would wake up and, on the good and bad days, read those prayers. No matter what, I made up my mind that I was going to open that journal.

There is a beautiful enemy to our feelings, and it's called faith. Faith is and should be the basis on which most of our belief system flows. Feeling like a fake and a fraud are what the devil whispers to distort the wonderful word of faith that God created and intended for us to believe and walk in. There are two things you can believe about yourself when you don't feel like praying and spending time with God:

1. I am a terribly lazy person who never makes time to do what I need to do.

2. I am a child of God. I'm human and living in a broken world. It's not that I don't want to but maybe it's that I don't know how to.

I am in no way saying there shouldn't be spontaneous moments with God. They're wonderful and they have shaped and directed my life for years. With that in mind, we must also accept that consistently reading a prayer in silence has just as much power in the spirit realm. Something supernatural happens when you push past your feelings and begin to pray.

Even though I felt like a fake reading those prayers, that practice would almost always push me into moments of real and genuine encounter with God. If you've ever been on a sports team, there's a reason you did warm-ups before the game. Once it was time to begin, the warms-ups and practices are what made the difference.

Rituals or routines should not be our entire prayer life, but there is nothing wrong with them being a part of it. I always say that we as people of faith are not always the most practical. We really do believe and trust God's Word; we just make it way too complicated. We want to run through religious and traditional hurdles when God is simply asking us to speak. He desires for us to open up to Him, anytime and anywhere, to daily pray His perfect will over our lives and those around us. Scripture clearly tells us to have the faith of a child. Children (although complex at times) are for the most part simple in practice and behavior. They are predictable, easily impressed, and always up for an adventure. May we be the same.

Okay, Jordan, I hear you and fully agree that there's an importance of meditating and thinking about my life. But why do I have to pray to God? Can't I just work really hard or speak and manifest my own thoughts?

If you've spent any time on customer-service calls with a large company, I bet at least once you've asked to talk to a manager. The person you're talking to could be delightful and kind, but you're still not getting anywhere with your overdue bill. The reason is that you need to speak to someone who has the power to actually do something. On customer-service calls, there are people who hear a no from the representative and never take the next step to ask for a manager. They didn't get the discount you got, not because they didn't deserve it but because of who they were talking to.

Talking to your friends about your problems without God is kind of like that call. They will listen, they will care, but their power is limited. I am not diminishing the power of accountability and community, but that cannot be the only foundation for our hopes and prayers.

Praying to God positions you to talk with the One who has the power not just to do something but also to do anything. We talk to people about our problems all day every day, so prayer is really not that different. We have made it our practice to put in our earbuds to talk to someone while walking the dog, shopping at the store, or driving down the road. We have implemented the habit of listening to a podcast or sermon a day when we have free time.

We spend too much time talking to the people who can change nothing instead of to God, who can change everything. Part of why we struggle with consistency in prayer is that we simply have bad information. My people perish, not for a lack of skill or goodness, but from a lack of knowledge. Have you ever found a truth in Scripture and it was like it solved a few of your frustrations at once? For me it was when I read that faith is the opposite of sight. In my old thinking, if I couldn't see, I would freak out. I would panic or begin to worry about the worst possible outcome.

Now when I can't see, because I have the truth of Scripture, I simply see it as a cue to activate my God-given faith muscles. I can begin to daily work out the truths I've found in the Scriptures.

I hope this truth of your feelings can unlock a new practice for you, that every time you think, *I really don't feel like* _____, you are filled with excitement because you now know what to do.

"Well, I don't know what to pray today."

Great, do you know God? Has God ever done anything for you? Talk about Him, proclaim His goodness, and thank Him for all He's done.

"I don't have any problems today."

Consider the world, all those who are less fortunate around you. We are to get to a point in our faith journey when life is no longer all about us.

"I can fix these things myself."

I bet you probably can! We should invite God into all things. He is the creator after all.

We have developed a strict belief system of when and how we can pray. My grandma made me repeat that prayer at dinner. It was so drawn out and I'd space out midway through, thinking about how I really just wanted that fried chicken in front of me.

Our parents had us kneel beside our bed at night and put our hands together. None of these traditions are bad; they were meant to help us, not keep us. They were a starting place, but far too often we have made them the only experience with Him. This guide intends to strip things down to the bare necessities, to talk about what prayer is, but also what it is not. A few friends have asked me why some days I start my day with just one prayer. Well, I truly believe that one prayer, the right prayer, has the ability to radically change everything.

"Prayer does not mean simply to pour out one's heart. It means rather to find the way to God and to speak with him, whether the heart is full or empty."

—Dietrich Bonhoeffer

Something super natural happens when you push past your feelings and begin to pray

III. ENCOUNTER

You won't get very far in prayer if you are speaking to someone who doesn't really exist to you. For most people, prayer feels like a great big toss-up. We occasionally and desperately offer our thoughts to the heavens in hopes that someone may be listening. Prayer is at the forefront of our brains when we need it and forgotten when we don't.

Over the years I have had many indescribable encounters with God in my prayer time. As amazing as they were, they would not have existed had I not had the first encounter. When I was on a missions trip in New Orleans right after hurricane Katrina, I had a genuine and life-changing encounter with Jesus. We went to rebuild houses, and God somehow did the same in me. I didn't know what was happening, but God used my new environment, the nearness of suffering, and lending a healing hand to open me up to Him. You don't need to find your grandma's God or your neighbor's religion; you need an experience with the God of the Bible, the King who will be Lord over your life.

You may not be blinded like Paul on the road to Damascus, going from killing Christians to saving them, but you will have an encounter and you will begin to change.

Jesus is the great teacher. He doesn't just tell us what to do; He shows us. His life, recorded in the Gospels, in all of its splendor, leads us to change. We simply cannot follow Him and stay the same.

Prayer is a daily encounter with the creator of the universe, not based solely on feeling but rooted in consistency and pushed forward by intimacy. Prayer moves us from a one-time experience to a daily encounter. What we got once by the encounter, we can now walk in every day.

Intimacy is not always cultivated by a routine or a checklist but often by your availability—the amount of time you're open to saying yes to God in a day. The question is not, are you smart enough, good enough, or pretty enough; it is, are you willing? Your faith journey begins with one simple moment of saying yes. After this first encounter, the relationship is strengthened by your willingness to daily surrender your time and attention to Him.

To be clear, anyone can pray to God. It's the deep intimacy and communion with the Father that will be scarce before a true encounter with Jesus. A new encounter with God, for the saint and the unbeliever, starts with the feeling of being somewhere new. Maybe you go to a Justin Bieber concert because you're a fan and midway through he begins to sing a song about Jesus. He brings out another guest singer and you all of a sudden find yourself in tears and with chills up your arm.

You're scrolling YouTube and somehow come across Maverick City Music. It's in your suggested list, so why not click it? Chills go up your body and you can't look away even if you want to. You wonder, *What is happening? Why do I feel this way?*

Maybe you're out for a weekend coffee and pastry. You run into that friend from school who you know was that "kind Christian." They begin to ask you questions that no one asks. You open up and share more than you intended to share.

Now here is the true test. When you experience this new feeling, do you feel peace? Do you feel safe, seen, and loved? Are your troubles and insecurities no longer in the forefront of your mind? I'd say you might just be in the presence of God.

Often times many of us in religious circles are afraid to discuss feelings and emotions. God is the creator of both. He then perfectly lived and expressed both in the world through Jesus. We should not fear our feelings, but we also should not bow to them when they are of the flesh. God will use them as often as we allow Him to. We should learn to appreciate them but not rely on them. I don't have to feel Him to serve Him, and I don't have to touch Him to know He's there.

> Is there anyplace I can go to avoid your Spirit?
> to be out of your sight?
> If I climb to the sky, you're there!
> If I go underground, you're there!
> If I flew on morning's wings
> to the far western horizon,
> You'd find me in a minute —
> you're already there waiting!
> (Psalm 139:8-11)

Another translation of Psalm 139 says, "If I make my bed in hell." I've had a few of those moments in my story. To make my bed in hell is the opposite of a good feeling; it's a dark place, especially when my own decisions lead me there. The end of verse 12 comforts us when our feelings don't quite line up with God's goodness. "It's a fact: darkness isn't dark to you; night and day, darkness and light, they're all the same to you." (Psalm 139:12) Even when we can't see, our Father can. In moments when I don't feel Him, His Word promises me that He's there!

If feelings are the focus of your prayer life, then you won't even make it out of the parking lot. At least 50 percent of my time with God looks like, "I don't feel it this morning, but I'm going to do it anyway."

There will almost always be a point of resistance when we sit down to talk with God. There's a reason you feel push-back when you think about going to the gym, because it's good for you! Your body and flesh are not so keen on being put in their place. With God, Adam and Eve ruled over the garden; it wasn't the other way around.

If you've ever gone to a chiropractor, you know it's all about setting things back into place. As we move about in life, parts of our ecosystem come out of alignment. That backstabbing friend causes us to now live guarded. The abuse or neglect cause us to no longer trust authority. That bad experience with a church leads to us resisting real community.

Time with God may be an encounter, but it's always an alignment. It aligns the part of us that "wasn't feeling it," when we would rather get on with our day. The chiropractor aligns my back; God sets right my spirit. Prayer puts my heart in line with His. When I am out of alignment with God, I tend to not treat others like I want to be treated. I so quickly store away what I've been taught about loving like Jesus, and I start loving like me. My encouraging voice becomes critical and negative.

I may live in a wicked world, but I also serve a holy God. When I choose to walk with Him, I begin to leave this world to focus on the heavenly kingdom to come. Even though it's not time to go yet, my eyes are set on that appointed time.

C. S. Lewis said, "If I find in myself a desire which no experience in this world can satisfy, the most probable explanation is that I was made for another world." This is not our home; we are just passing through. While living in a broken world, surrounded by our stress and worries, it's such an easy thing to forget. Time with Him reminds me of how good He has been and how good He always will be.

> "If you'll hold on to me for dear life," says God,
>   "I'll get you out of any trouble.
> I'll give you the best of care
>   if you'll only get to know and trust me.
> Call me and I'll answer, be at your side in bad times;
>   I'll rescue you, then throw you a party.
> I'll give you a long life,
>   give you a long drink of salvation!"
> (Psalm 91:14-16)

Scripture often reminds me that there may be troubles but I am not alone. The devil's lies ring truer the further away you are from God. The devil can drown us in insecurity, comparison, and emotional distress if we never hear the words our Father speaks about us.

He has also convinced a generation of people who God is, and they've never even met Him. Most of the people around you don't dislike God; they are just resisting their idea of Him. You can believe the lies about me until you get to know me. The closer you get, the more truth you will experience. You can read papers about me, hear secondhand stories, and collect half-truths surrounding my name. But until you take me to coffee, enter my home for dinner, or go on my morning run, you won't actually know me.

Have the powers of darkness convinced an entire generation of who God is in hopes that they won't find out the truth? If we dig deeper, have the enemy's lies convinced an entire group of Christians who God is in hopes that we won't give Him everything?

In situations where I have no control, I know someone who does. No matter how hard I try, I cannot be like Him without first being with Him. More is caught than taught, and most of us have heard a lot of teaching. There are some things that we can only catch by being with Him.

I love the words from the song "Pilgrim" by John Mark McMillan:

> There is a heavenly city
> That I'm compelled to find
> Though I love the flowers and trees
> And the smell of the grinding sea
> And all the beautiful things here in life
> I, I'm a pilgrim here
> On this side of the great divide
> I'm a pilgrim here
> But I'll walk with you for a while

If we are truly souls living in a temporary world, we must carve out time for the eternal; we must make room so that the part of us that will never die can truly live. Heaven is a place, but it's also a person—a person who is fully accessible, not if He makes time for us, but if we make time for Him. Oh, my prayer is that we get to the end of our life and have made time for the God who will carry our souls from Earth to eternity!

There is nothing wrong with a hopeful expectancy of heaven, as long as we are not neglecting His presence today. We can have all of God today! We have been offered all of Him, but will He get all of us?

It's easy to get discouraged and wonder if we're doing all of this right. *Have I had an encounter? How do I go about having more of them? I don't think I can hear God talking back.* We must learn to ignore and resist the voices of insecurity. God is a rewarder of those who patiently wait. Not only that, but God consistently acts favorably to those who step in faith and simply try their best—like the woman who brought all she had into the temple: others brought more, but she gave all she had.

Other people may have more experience with God, possess more knowledge, and can quote more scriptures, but *you have to just be you.* To me, that's about as close as it gets to being naked in the garden with Adam and Eve—bringing your true and authentic self to God. He will honor and reward the best you can bring.

Perfection is for heaven, transformation
is for now. Heaven is my home,
but it begins here today.

Prayer is a daily encounter
with the creator of
the Universe

IV. PLAN

Over the next few days, whether you have an amazing prayer life or a nonexistent one, I believe this book has the ability to help get you going. For those of you with a rich history with God, I pray this will continue to awaken what already exists. In no way do I want to downgrade the importance of prayer, in practice or in wording. As we start on this journey together, I want to speak more specifically on the subject of talking to God.

Most of us have been taught that there are certain moments, places, and rituals that we must practice when we pray. We were told to kneel by our bed, close our eyes, recite specific words or phrases. I remember getting in trouble with prayer as a kid at my great-grandmother's. I picked up my glass during the prayer and you could hear the ice jingle around. I'm not against reverence or focus in prayer, and the people who taught us meant well. The ancient concepts and teachings of prayer may be old but they're not useless.

I get bored if I have to read the same bible translation all the time. I have my primary one, but then I will search for other translations to see how things were interpreted. I often learn and experience fresh things with a quick look at a newer translation. The methods, wording, and style of Scripture have changed as language has evolved, so shouldn't the practice of prayer be the same? The Bible itself did not change; the way we consume it did. I have nothing against the King James Version or other older translations, but it's hard to go from speaking in real life to reading that. It can be done but it doesn't feel as seamless as one of the newer versions.

Prayer is holy and full of awestruck wonder, but it is also a conversation. You don't have to talk normal to your friends and then become some different person with God. Many of us turn into people from ancient kingdoms when it's time to pray. *Thou, oh Lord, You hath bestowed upon us Your glorious presence. Give us Thy sunrise again tomorroweth and keepeth my toes from stumbling in the briar patch. Be with Thy wayward souls who are drunketh at midday. Until tomorrow. Goodbyeth, Lord.*

He knows you better than you know Him. So be yourself.

After our time is up, my hope is that you see this book more like a daily tool and less like a one-time read. The sections exist to help certain types of people stay on track. A great deal of thought went into the placement of the collections, but they also stand on their own. I hope you're enveloped and encouraged as you read for the first time. I also hope you pick it up again a year from now when your prayer life feels off.

When starting this project, my heart was never for me to teach you the perfect way to pray. I'm not sure any human could claim to do that one. In a weird way, as this guide breaks the traditional "ritual" of prayer, I hope that you find a new one—your own tradition, a process, rhythm, and space that work for you and your daily life. Simply put, if it doesn't work for you, you won't do it. And there is so much power and possibility when you do.

"Good planning and hard work lead to prosperity, but hasty shortcuts lead to poverty."

Proverbs 21:5

We spend too much time talking to the people who can change nothing instead of to God, who can change everything.

Prayer is holy and full of awestruck wonder, but it is also a conversation.

V. PRACTICAL

Do you know why we often refuse to believe that things are simple? Because then we'd have to do them! Let's zoom out to the 10,000-foot view for a moment. If there is a greater being called God, if He did make this thing called Earth, and we are the beings He formed to live on it, the most reasonable thought would be that because of His deity and our humanity, we would daily make our request known to Him in prayer.

If we are what we are, and God is who He is, then prayer is the most natural response in the entire Bible. I love reading Scripture, I enjoy singing to my favorite songs, I am honored to serve and to give, but for me, talking to God has become the most effortless. Notice I did not say easy, but once you finally begin, effortless.

In Bible times, the priest would have to go into God's presence and pray *for* you. There was a barrier in between you and God. Your priest was interceding for you, your family, and your community. His sacrifice counted as yours. Jesus came, lived, and died, and it ruined the religious practices of the day. Jesus cut out the middle man for God's people. Jesus took on the responsibility of the cross so that we could pick up a life of prayer. Where a priest or sacrifice was once required, Jesus now fills the gap. He made a way where tradition and ritual were not only preferred but required.

At the day of Pentecost, after Jesus had returned to heaven, the Holy Spirit fell upon the people gathered. The same power that raised Christ from the dead was now in them. The great High Priest had been beside them, doing miracles, signs, and wonders. But in an unbelievable turn of events, they now had the power that Jesus had. Simply put, the Holy Spirit is the spirit of God on the earth. The work of the Spirit didn't stop after Bible times; He's still at work in believers today. I could write an entire book on the Holy Spirit; just know that His role in our life of prayer is just as significant as Jesus and the Father.

The Holy Spirit is the nearness of God. He comforts me when I'm lonely, speaks when I'm lost, and fills me with peace at just the right time. To say the Holy Spirit is the opposite of what it was like to have a priest would be an understatement.

Has our newfound access to God created complacency in our hearts? We must pause and be grateful for what we now have in prayer. Everything comes at a cost, even if we didn't pay for it.

The more you come to understand prayer, the less it feels like a chore and the more it feels like an opportunity. Tragedy, worry, disappointment, and fear aren't going anywhere; the only difference is that we now have a connection to the King. His people don't have to call your people. When you choose Jesus, you become His, and He is yours.

One thing I want to make clear is that we as believers all have this direct line to God. If you have accepted Christ, then there is nothing that stands between you and the Creator.

> So then, since we have a great High Priest
> who has entered heaven,
> Jesus the Son of God, let us hold firmly to what we believe.
> This High Priest of ours understands our weaknesses,
> for he faced all of the same testings we do, yet he did not sin.
> So let us come boldly to the throne of our gracious God.
> There we will receive his mercy, and we will find grace
> to help us when we need it most.
> (Hebrews 4:14-16)

Just because we have access does not mean that we all recognize or take advantage of it. I bet that 95 percent of things you complain or gossip about would make great prayers. The enemy is so deceiving, he wants to get you to voice daily the things you should be bringing before God. Someone once said that God doesn't answer your complaints. Test it out: for the next week, when you go to voice negativity or thoughts to yourself or others, see if you can turn them into prayers. Make it a challenge! Anyone can gossip or speak what is most obvious. (We all have done it.)

It takes a mature follower of Jesus to speak life and hope over situations that seem to have none.

> I can't believe they're getting a divorce.
> Did you see her mugshot?
> I think their son deals drugs.
> I'm always depressed.
> I'm too broke to do that.
> We'll see if they can stick to following Jesus.

I never get anything from going to church.
I don't have time to read and pray.

When you gossip and complain, you are a part of the problem. When you pray, you become a part of the answer.

I can't believe they're getting a divorce.

I pray that You would restore their family and their marriage. Give them hope and peace during this time.

Did you see her mugshot?

I'm believing that this moment would turn her toward You, that she would feel Your overwhelming love and grace today.

I think their son deals drugs.

I pray that You would give them peace tonight; remind them that You are the healer, redeemer, and savior.

I'm always depressed.

God, I ask that You would give me a new joy in my heart. Help me to focus on the positive things that are happening for me.

I'm too broke to do that.

God, I ask for breakthrough in my finances. May I never again be limited when I want to be generous with others.

We'll see if they can stick to following Jesus.

God, I ask that You would sustain them in their recent step of faith! Show me how I and others can support them on their new journey. Give them strength to not turn back to their old ways.

I never get anything from going to church.

Prepare my heart to receive Your Word and step into community. Strengthen and encourage our pastor as he prepares the word.

I don't have time to read and pray.

Help me to see the places in my life where I waste time. Place in my heart a new hunger for worship and the Word.

I am guilty of saying all of these and many more, but with a shift in perspective they can all become prayers. Every prayer has the potential to move God's heart; then things begin to change.

The fact that your first thought is negative does not make you a bad person. It means you're broken; we all are broken thanks to the fall of man. We are not held accountable for our random thoughts, but we are responsible for what we do with them.

We all have had the urge to pick up the phone and gossip. You sometimes have to say out loud, "Nope, I'm not going there today. I'm not allowing this way of thinking into my space and my day."

The practicality in prayer is that it's a simple shift in the way that we already think and speak. The situations are still not good, but you now have a direct line to the One who is. If you go from feeling helpless to having power, you can't help but look at the bad and see the good, look at the dark and see the light. Seeing potential in yourself and in others is the very heart of Christ. Kindness is not just what He does because He feels sympathy for us; it's who He is. Prayer doesn't just affect you; it has the potential to change everyone around you.

Emboldened in prayer, you begin to believe that the prodigal is soon to come home. The sick family member may very well be healed. The new job opportunity is around the corner.

I know you can think of a scenario where someone you know left the church and they no longer trust in God. It's that helpless feeling of knowing they're going down the wrong path and there's nothing you can do about it. When I find out about these scenarios, I almost always say the same thing: "God's hand may actually be on their life." I always get funny looks. "Jordan, did you hear? I just said my brother no longer trusts in God and he's going down the wrong path." Yeah, but he knows the way home; there's hope for him in Jesus.

This is not a name-it-and-claim-it moment or a product of my delusion. This is, *I used to have my own eyes, but now I see people like He does.* The only reason I have this perspective is because I was a prodigal son myself. I reached a place of questioning God in my early 20s. It was a slow process but I ended up ignoring the things of God for many years. When I left the church, there were plenty of negative voices adding to the wave that pushed me away. Most people viewed me only by my actions, which by nature requires the least effort, and no faith. Thankfully, there were a few people who saw me like Jesus. Even while I was still running, they pulled me back in. They spoke life, showed love, and prayed over my potential and my future. Make no mistake, I was full on "Jonah running from

Nineveh"—thankfully without the whale. Nothing I was doing in the physical would have given these people hope; they were seeing me like God did.

Prayer is practical because it works, plain and simple. Faith is the opposite of sight. A prerequisite to needing faith is the existence of unbelief. We should not be so surprised when those without faith also carry unbelief. There are people or even places in your own life that seem hopeless. Are you seeing things with your physical eyes or with your eyes of faith? Don't overthink how to do this, or sit around wondering if you're doing it right. These things already occupy your brain space. They are constantly playing like a recording in your head. I could aim to tell you where to start exercising your faith, but chances are you've already got plenty of openings.

You have a list of things you could gossip, worry, or complain about. This whole practice of talking with God may seem too good to be true, but there's only one way to find out.

"Remember, it is sin to know what you
 ought to do and then not do it"

James 4:17

When you gossip and complain, you are
a part of the problem; when you pray,
you become a part of the answer.

Jesus took on the responsibility
of the cross so that we
could pick up a life of prayer.

VI. GIFT

One morning I thought, *What's one of the greatest gifts God has ever given me?* If you are super spiritual you might say Jesus, and that would be true. I believe I was unknowingly searching for something a bit different here. I sat for a few minutes and journaled "your mornings." One of the best gifts God has ever given me is my mornings?! I had to ponder this one, I'm not going to lie! The more I thought about it, the more I remembered how much I loved the start of the day. On a very natural level, my brain and body are fresh, I'm excited to wake up and start my day with reading a writing. I love the afternoon and the evening, but I believe the biggest differentiator about the mornings is that it happens first.

We see throughout Scripture a consistent pattern of God asking for the first from His people: the first sacrifice, the first tithe, the first fruits. Even God gave His first and only Son, Jesus. Doing something first always requires faith. If we are speaking in terms of spending time with God, it takes faith to say, *I'm going to do this first, before I see how my day is going to go. I'm going to trust God that if I put Him at the first of my day, the rest will be blessed. I'm going to pray this prayer over my lost friend, without knowing the outcome of their life.* I'm deciding to be generous before my next paycheck.

Some scholars and pastors would even call this the principle of the first. I like to say that when you choose to do something first, there's a little something extra on it. Principles in Scripture are like keys, and when you use them, doors tend to open. We are stepping into God's operating system, which means we have to act accordingly. We live, eat, work, and play in the world that God created. We can attempt to do it our own way, but Scripture tells us time and again that it only leads to destruction. Since we are in God's kingdom, we have to understand our part. We can easily quote the promises of God without realizing that a command or principle is tied to it. We have to walk in the principle in order to claim our promise.

For example, we always quote, "I'm the head and not the tail, above and not beneath." Let's look at the whole verse:

> If you *listen* to these commands of the Lord your God that I am giving you today, and if you carefully *obey* them, *the Lord will make you the head and not the tail,* and you will always be on top and never at the bottom. (Deuteronomy 28:13)

Listen -> Obey -> Then

It doesn't say that your hard work, great attitude, or new spouse will help you get ahead—the Lord alone will make you the head and not the tail. This whole promise may end on the mountaintop, but it starts with listening. Many choose to ignore His voice in certain areas, numbing the conscience to an unwillingness to obey. We all want the promise, blessing, and long life, but are we willing to submit to the Lord over them? *"God is not a man, so he does not lie. He is not human, so he does not change his mind. Has he ever spoken and failed to act? Has he ever promised and not carried it through?" (Numbers 23:19).*

Between meetings, social media, and lunch with friends, the longer the day continues, the more noise tends to fill our brain. It's only reasonable to conclude that the time of the day with the least noise is the easiest time to hear and receive from God. God is not bound by time, but we are, so we must look at our lives and find what works. I am well aware that everyone is not a morning person like me. If we want to practice what we are learning, I would suggest simply asking God to help you be energized and wake up earlier. I am not implying that you must spend hours in prayer first thing in the morning (although it would not be frowned upon). What I am saying for certain is that you should do something, and you should do it first.

There are times when I have over an hour with Him in the morning. Other days I only have 30 minutes. He honors your plan and your genuine effort to keep it. When I first wake up in the morning, I start my day by saying out loud, "Good morning, Lord. Thank You."

This simple arrangement of words acknowledges God and reminds me why I woke up and ultimately why I am here. Notice I didn't say "God"—I said "Lord." this places Him as Lord over my life and over my day. *"Listen to my voice in the morning, Lord. Each morning I bring my requests to you and wait expectantly" (Psalm 5:3).*

Mornings are quiet, the light is dim, and the coffee is fresh; it is the perfect moment to pause and take things in a bit longer. Even with all of the enjoyable things that the morning brings, it is also the easiest time of the day to rush past. It is natural to look at what's next on the schedule instead of penciling in more time to be mindful. I recently asked some friends to take three deep breaths with me. That's about 15 seconds. They looked at me like I was a little crazy! When was the last time you had 15 seconds when you thought and did nothing?

A deep breath in God's presence can go a long way. When I start my day with God, I am not guaranteed a perfect day, but I am making up my mind. I am predetermining not what will happen to me but how strong and centered I will be when it's time to respond.

Prayer is the conscious choice to no longer walk alone. I have no idea what will happen to me at work or school, but I know who will be with me when it does. To be clear, God is very much with you, everywhere and all of the time. Prayer seems to give us a deeper awareness to this reality.

When I align myself with God's heart, it prepares me for the unknown. I do not know what is to come, but because of the gift of my mornings, I now have a better grasp on how to handle it.

Sadly, we often put talking to God on our chore list; we add it as a line item on our sticky note. It is a lot more like opening a gift: first the bow, then tearing off the paper, and then opening the box. Each day it is different; each day it is essential and custom-tailored just for you.

God is not out of touch. He does not send you oversized clothing like your aunt from Connecticut. He does not give you books you care nothing about or movies you have already seen. He loves you, and He knows you even better than you know yourself. The good gifts are waiting—the playbooks, blueprints, and the glimmers of hope—not if you are good, but if you simply choose to slow down and open them.

"Let me hear of your unfailing love each morning, for I am trusting you. Show me where to walk, for I give myself to you"

Psalm 143:8

Yes, God is listening to every single one
of your prayers.

Good morning Lord.
Thank you.

VII. PLACE

God is the strongest and most powerful person we will ever have the privilege of knowing. He can raise the dead, push back the powers of darkness, and burn up an entire city with one command. With the grandness of God, why do we often have trouble finding Him in our own lives?

God is loud, He is strong, but He is also in the whisper. He never misses you, but you can easily miss Him. In our overstimulated and hectic lives, we have yet to establish a place for Him. If your body is in good shape, you have a place you get it into that condition. If your mind is constantly stimulated and learning, then you have an area where you sit and read.

Someone once said, "No one ever drifts to a good place." Intentionality doesn't just happen; you plan for it and get results.

If your friends are coming over, you put in extra preparation in the part of the house where you'll be hosting them. We have plenty of space for the things that don't fully transform our soul, and yet somehow we seem to be too overwhelmed to create a space for Him. God's presence used to be in one place: the priests were the only ones privileged (and "clean") enough to make their way into the temple. People like you and me would hope to hear something from their experience, or maybe hear the Scriptures read every so often. They did not get what we have now: the glory we have comfortably grown accustomed to. "I tell you, many prophets and kings longed to see what you see, but they didn't see it. And they longed to hear what you hear, but they didn't hear it" (Luke 10:24).

It's hard to know what it feels like to go without something we've always had. When Jesus died, it unleashed His life-giving presence to all of us. The veil that once kept us out was now split open to let us in. "The light from the sun was gone. And suddenly, the curtain in the sanctuary of the Temple was torn down the middle" (Luke 23:45).

I'm afraid that the more available His presence became, the more complacent we grew. The presence left the ark, and it undoubtedly finds a home in so many believers around the world. It is open to all who are willing to humbly submit to God. We must all consider, has it found a home in us?

After the veil was torn in the temple, the priests tried to mend the veil and put it back up. I often wonder, have we done the same in our lives? Would we rather God be at a distance so we can enjoy our many desires and ambitions? Are we trying to sew back the veil keeping us from God's presence now that we've found it? How often we are willing to stay stuck in our current season instead of experiencing the freedom of the next one.

You must establish a place, not just for Him, but for you—a space that when you sit, prop your feet up, and open your journal, life stands still. You can pray anywhere and everywhere; God will reach you if He wants to reach you. I believe that finding your place is a practice that will set you up for the best possible outcome. It's going to happen in other places, but it's going to happen more consistently when you intentionally create a space for Him.

Here are just a few of my favorite preferences for my space with God:

Quiet
Private
Peaceful
Phone-free
Journal open
Something to drink
Near the warm sunlight

How would you prepare your home for a guest coming to visit? You'd clean up, light a candle, turn on some background music, and expectantly wait by the window. You'd welcome them in, offer a drink, and even show them where they can sit. Developing our place is the starting point, actually using it is where the magic happens. God doesn't need to know where to meet you, but you need to know where to consistently meet Him. He's not bound by time or place, but we often are.

Although I have office hours, certain days of the week are more flexible for me than others. If I try to "work from home" in my bed, my brain just wants to go to sleep. I have to resist the urge to get in bed. I must stay at my desk in my office if I plan to get things done. As you develop places of peace in your home or property, you'll quickly find those places that may not be best.

Your place with God doesn't need to be Instagram-able. You don't have to spend $300 at Target before God will come. The Bible has a comforting promise: it's that wherever we go, He will be with us. I'm not attempting to put God in a box; He is omnipresent. I do however know that I'm more consistent when there's order, when I have a safe and quiet place to sit and reflect on God and all that He has done. There are a wide range of coffee shops in the city where I live. All of them have great coffee and most of them have friendly service. I can't explain why, but there's one shop where I feel an overwhelming peace. Although I have my place at home, I know that shop is another place with Him. I can go there and easily feel what I experience in my spot at home.

As with any practice, we are not to become legalistic; some rules are meant to be broken. Meet with Him at home, but there will be days when you will want to go to the park or the outdoor shop nearby. No matter how many physical places we set up shop to meet with God, I want you to remember that God's presence is in and around you, not just today but every day. The place where He truly dwells is in us. *"Look! I stand at the door and knock. If you hear my voice and open the door, I will come in, and we will share a meal together as friends" (Revelation 3:20).*

How long would you let your dinner guest stand outside and wait? Shouldn't we treat God with even more care? No matter how many physical places we create, God's presence is in you and around you. You are the carrier of the goodness of God, and that begins with sitting in your place with Him.

"How can we lead people into the quiet place beside still waters if we are in constant motion?"

—Eugene Peterson

The veil that once kept us out was now split open to let us in.

VIII. SILENCE

If you are dwelling with God and being kept by Him, there is a place you reach in the road that you might not expect. It's a moment when God goes quiet. It's the place where you have prayed and prayed some more and there is still no answer. There are many, many reasons why God is silent to our prayer requests. And I will not pretend to know how to deal with each and every scenario.

I want to say clearly that I believe God speaks to us; we should seek His guidance and even wait for His response. I had been praying for weeks about if God wanted me to move back to Tennessee. I knew that I was pretty sure it was what God wanted, but I hadn't heard from Him clearly. I pressed in, prayed, and journaled for weeks but never got a direct yes or no. It was in this moment that I realized God was relying on me, as a mature follower of Jesus, to make my own decision.

I recently listened to an interview with Charles Stanley and his son Andy Stanley. Andy was talking to his dad about parenting and his career as a pastor. He shared how as kids, his dad would never make decisions for them. His dad would always tell them to pray about it and make their own decision. Charles's kids were barely teenagers and he was putting the world in their hands. Here's what Charles said about it: "People learn to make decisions when you refuse to make them for them."

Andy is now a pastor and has written books, recorded podcasts, and spoken at conferences all centered around leadership. Andy now feels that, as a pastor and leader, one of his refined skills is decision making, and he relates it back to his father's parenting. Could God be doing the same with us? If you are living life led by the Spirit and trusting in God, maybe, just maybe, God trusts you to make the decision this time! At times, God has spoken all He is going to speak until we make our first step.

We can also embrace silence with the truth that our relationship with God isn't based solely on words or feelings. In most human relationships, we may experience silence and think something is wrong. We might receive a short one-word text and then wonder if everything is okay. I remember my mentor Daniel telling me that he and his friend would meet up for tea, each grab a book, and sit silently for hours. I immediately thought, *What? You mean you guys could sit there in silence and think everything is okay?*

It could be due to our age difference—that accepting silence comes a little more naturally to Daniel. Even with quieter individuals, silence doesn't feel normal to many of us living in the internet age. It is quite shocking to realize that God is waiting on us in some scenarios. We also understand that His silence doesn't necessarily represent any anger or distance from us. If we dig to the root of the issue, we find our own severe discomfort with silence. If I were reading this chapter, I would probably say something like, "But I really enjoy being alone; this isn't me!" Being alone and sitting in silence are two very different things. I can be by myself and still be mentally stimulated by podcasts, YouTube videos, books, and music—all of which I enjoy and approve of, but not when silence is needed. Peter Scazzero so brilliantly explains this phenomenon in his book *Emotionally Healthy Spirituality*: "Ignoring our emotions is turning our back on reality. Listening to our emotions ushers us into reality. And reality is where we meet God."

We effectively avoid our emotions and true self by doing godly things. We listen to a sermon instead of searching the Scriptures. We turn on a podcasts or worship recording instead of sitting in the quiet. When we feel lonely, we hopelessly attempt to connect on social media or at in-person gatherings. None of the "godly" things above are bad; we just can't attempt to religiously practice them without Him.

God is found in the silent moments of our existence. He can and will break through all of the noise that we surround ourselves with, but He longs for the quiet moments with us. Scripture explains God as a jealous lover—not an evil kind of jealous, but the kind of joy you'd feel if your earthly relationships expressed jealousy out of love.

I believe God speaks more in some moments than others, but I'm certain that we can hear better when we're silent. So in the process of moving past our feelings to pray, we must also understand that there are positive ways to use our feelings. When practicing silence, the feeling of peace has become a close friend. To sit in silence for even 10 minutes early on in this practice felt like torture. As soon as I sat down, my mind would start to wander. You can start practicing silence by sitting in your quiet-time spot for 10-15 minutes a day. What I found to be effective was taking active moments to practice silence. Instead of listening to music in the shower, I'll turn it off. Instead of immediately turning on the podcast in the car, I'll take the first 10-15 minutes just to drive.

Silence should not feel like work, and you don't necessarily have to be still to practice it. You can simply take a moment when you may fill the quiet and rest in it. The more you do it, the more comfortable you'll feel with it. I will tell you now, the quieter you are, the more stillness you allow in your atmosphere, the more you will see and hear.

When I started practicing silence, I started to process my parents' divorce that happened almost a decade ago. I would have sworn on my life that I was good, that I was over it, that there was nothing left to deal with. I had thoughts of my grandpa passing away and even hurtful things that were said to me in school. God was taking me on the road less traveled, the quiet place to slow down, open up, and begin to heal. Even though silence first felt scary, His presence always brought me peace. As we uncovered the past, and even got direction for the future, He became the warmth right in the middle.

So how does all of this help us when God is truly silent to our request? Peace makes for an effective GPS when God is silent. I've heard pastors say this line as they were searching where to plant their church: "We just went to the south and drove around until we felt peace. Peace was our compass."

When God goes quiet, instead of being crippled I will just take a step and pause to see if I feel peace. The Holy Spirit is good at convicting us if we made a wrong turn. Often times when I take a step, and then another, I feel peace. If you're led by the Spirit, and you have a history with God, you will feel peace (or lack thereof) after making a decision. I don't mean "Does this decision feel good?" or "Am I happy?" When I lay my head down at night, do I feel peace inside about the direction I'm going and the choices I'm making?

I love what the author Francis Chan said about adoption: Why do we always wait for God to tell us to adopt children? Can't we read the Bible and know His heart for the orphan? What if we erred on the side of action as opposed to reluctancy? What if we took a step? Finally trusting our heart that He has been transforming?

Don't be afraid of silence! He meets us there. You are His beloved child, and good fathers begin to trust their children.

Elijah replied, "I have zealously served the Lord God Almighty. But the people of Israel have broken their covenant with you, torn down your altars, and killed every one of your prophets. I am the only one left, and now they are trying to kill me, too."

"Go out and stand before me on the mountain," the Lord told him. And as Elijah stood there, the Lord passed by, and a mighty windstorm hit the mountain. It was such a terrible blast that the rocks were torn loose, but the Lord was not in the wind. After the wind there was an earthquake, but the Lord was not in the earthquake. And after the earthquake there was a fire, but the Lord was not in the fire. And after the fire there was the sound of a gentle whisper" (1 Kings 19:10-12).

The whisper of God
Life may be simpler if we tune it out
But will it be better?
Elijah spent days
Looking at what was wrong
God called him out on the mountain
Not to correct or rebuke
Not to drop the gavel of judgment
To a place of silence
God passed by with gentleness
To heal, comfort, and restore
The truth is always with Him
Are we positioned to hear it?

Silence is beautiful and expansive.
When we are silent, we see ourselves
and we hear God. The more silent we
are, the more we see and hear Him. The
more noise, the less we see.

Dont be afraid of silence!
He meets us there.

IX. MEDITATION

My non-Christian friends will often ask me if I "meditate." I have never quite known how to respond as a follower of Jesus, as the focus of most conversation is prayer. I couldn't write this book on prayer without addressing something that's rising in popularity. There are apps, classes, social groups, and courses on how to properly meditate and find your quiet place. I genuinely love the branding and general wording of the meditation movement; slowing down, quieting the noise, and creating space for myself all sound great to me.

I struggled for weeks wondering what it means to be a Christian and meditate. I discovered that the commercialized version of meditation is simply prayer, without God. They are getting some of the benefits of prayer, silence, clarity, and peace, without God. This view of meditation is a work-around to try to get God's promise without God Himself. They are attempting to temporarily rest the soul without understanding that their eternal destinies hang in the balance. The truth will always be love, no matter how it is received. If this is you, there is no fear or condemnation over you. Opening this book and reading the Scriptures will show you that an invitation to prayer and godly meditation is *still available to you.*

So can we as followers of Jesus meditate in a Christian way? As I studied deeper, I found it to be a resounding *yes!* This excited me because I really do love the thought of meditation. Most people view meditation as clearing your mind; but as Christians, we must see meditation as filling our mind. "I will meditate on your precepts and fix my eyes on your ways" (Psalm 119:15).

Those who only meditate don't have the right things to fill their mind with. It's all about discarding the junk, clearing the mind, only to fill it with junk again. We as followers of Jesus are promised a river of life that will never run dry. When we come to God in prayer (submitting request) and meditation (filling ourselves with the things of God), we don't stop with clearing our mind of the bad. Anxiety, worry, fear, and depression can often take a heavy toll on the mind. There have been so many days when I felt like I couldn't get anything done.

Meditation is a medicine for the battles we face in our minds and our lives—but not just any type of meditation: biblical meditation. There are many things we could discuss, but I want to focus on three main ways I meditate as a follower of Jesus.

1. **Word**: Scripture is very clear that we are to meditate on the Word. The Bible tells me more than just the right and wrong things to do with my life. Scripture is often described as a mirror; it shows me who I am and also points me to who I can be in Christ. I am a new creation, with new promises and opportunities in my future. The day gives me things to

worry about; the Word gives me truths to believe in. We all have those voices that repeat the same negative stuff over and over in our brain. One way to combat this is to read scriptures that speak the truth of God against our doubts and insecurities. Meditating on scripture is less about quantity and more about quality. The young theologian Bonhoeffer would often meditate an entire week on one verse. The Puritans would take one verse and write a 300-page book. We cannot overlook one verse let alone one word; each is alive and filled with the breath of God.

2. **Thought**: Christian meditation is the best medicine for a lack of peace in your mind. *God, make these thoughts go away*—we have all prayed this prayer in frustration. God makes it clear in Scripture that we are to set our mind on things above. This is not from the Greek or Hebrew, but "to set" seems physical to me. "To set" something means you have to pick it up and then place it somewhere else. Something does not get moved passively but with force. Setting our mind is a conscious and strategic effort to dwell on something other than what we're naturally desiring. We cannot control the many thoughts that will enter our mind as we explore this fallen place. If the devil is speaking, then he's lying. Whatever things he's saying to you, know that there's a promise in Scripture that combats it. My thoughts are wild and free, but when I meditate on the truths of God, I have control. As I observe the beauty of creation around me, I feel His closeness and warmth. When I'm worried about something, I must chose to "set" my mind elsewhere.

I take back what the enemy tried to steal—my perfect peace.

3. **Worship**: In times of worship, I sing, lift my hands, clap, and even dance. I love how the music helps set the mood and aligns my heart with the moment. As much as I love worship music, some of my most beautiful moments with God have been in complete silence. Whether I'm in corporate worship or streaming online, I will often take a deep breath and clear my head. I make space for God to speak and to move in the moment. We have slowly moved away from one truth: worship is about God. It all centers around who He is, what He's done, and all He deserves. Someone once said, "You must be intentional because you never drift to a good place." There is nothing wrong with being open in worship, letting God move your thoughts and heart. We must be careful that it's God taking us somewhere and not ourselves. If I can't easily clear my mind, then I'll meditate and think about His goodness. I won't let my mind drift if I like the music, the lights, or the people. I'll praise and thank Him for who He is and all the good He has done in my life. Worship is about God, and that's something worth meditating on.

Self-love

One thing that's really helped me with meditation is to purchase a set of notecards or a journal. I suggest that you sit down and think through the things you most often hear in your head:

I'm not good enough.

My life isn't interesting.
I wish I looked different.
I always mess things up.
I'm lonely.

With your trusty tool Google, see if you can find verses that combat those voices in your head. We have learned to believe the voices we hear. Look for scriptures that speak of the nature and goodness of God. Write them down on paper using a pen, and meditate on them. Dare to speak them out loud when the voices of negativity come.

Loving Others

While there are days I feel down, there are also times when I'm prideful and focused only on myself. Once I become self-centered, I become hyper-focused on my problems, forgetting about everyone I'm called to walk with. When I get into this place, I'll often take another note card or my phone and write down names of people in my life:

Rich
Caleb
Abby
Jeremiah
Maddie
Daniel

If you simply think of the past few weeks, you can quickly remember people around you who need encouragement and prayer. When I'm struggling deeply in my mind, I'm almost always in a self-centered place. This process of praying for others lifts me above my situation and reminds me that life with Jesus is not all about me.

You are not fully responsible for what enters your mind; you are responsible for what stays.

"Since you have been raised to new
life with Christ, set your sights on the
realities of heaven, where Christ sits in
the place of honor at God's right hand.
Think about the things of heaven, not the
things of earth."

Colossians 3:1-2

Meditation is a medicine
for the battles we face in
our minds and our lives.

X. RHYTHM

For most of my life I was convinced that I was an extrovert. Through and through, I love people, I need the energy, and I feed off the crowd. I was soon corrected by friends that I'm actually an introverted extrovert. Which basically means, when I'm home I want to be home, but once I'm out, I can't get enough of it. I love new experiences, but I recharge at home alone.

There's a large part of me that loves to be at home on the couch with a good book. I light my candles, make tea, and sit with my dogs. There is the comfort and natural flow of my space at home. I don't have to settle in; I'm already there. The sights, smells, and sounds are not just there; they are mine. They belong to the space where I rest, reflect, and recharge.

The beauty about my newfound personality type is that I have found so much rest at home in this previous season. The introverted side of me doesn't resist the rhythms of rest. The extroverted side of my personality will sporadically decide to come to life when I'm out in public. I was recently attending a wedding and found myself on the dance floor. I looked over to my friend and said, "I need to save my energy for when my song comes on." He asked, "What's your song?" I laughed and replied, "I'm not sure but I'll know when it hits."

At any dance party, when each song ends, you turn your ear up and glance over at the DJ to hear what's next. If it's a good song, you keep up the fist pumping, if it's not, you walk off and take a water break. The bride's mom had requested the classic song "Rolling on the River." I was mildly clapping along and watching all the middle-aged women swinging their arms like windmills. Slowly as the beat began to pick up, my body started to respond, faster and faster. I felt it in my bones. This was my song, and it was happening. Like a lightning bolt, I found myself in the middle of the dance floor, dancing so hard I felt like my heart was going to beat out of my body. I even put my glasses on the bride's face so they wouldn't fall off me and break.

You could say I found the rhythm and I jumped into it. I wasn't thinking about my worries, insecurities, or tasks at work. I was having the time of my life. There may be beats in a song, but there are also rhythms to prayer. If you're a follower of Jesus, I believe you'll resonate with this. It is a very difficult thing to gauge, but in its simplest form, you're either in the rhythm or out of it. You're either on your seventh morning of consistent prayer and reading, or you're not exactly sure what got you off the rhythm a few weeks ago.

I'm really glad that you read the description of my dance moves and didn't actually see them in person. I'm not a good dancer. I knew I wasn't very good long before I hit the dance floor, so it made for a much better time. There's a joke I heard once about older people who play golf: "Although it's retirement, the only ones really having fun are the ones who know they aren't any good." Prayer becomes more enjoyable when you accept that you don't know that much about it and you aren't that good at it. What does being "good" at prayer mean anyway?

You know why it's disappointing to shop all day and come home with no bags? For most people, the point of shopping is not solely to people-watch, eat a salty pretzel, or burn calories walking around in your cargo shorts. The reason you go is to bring something home. If we are not careful, we use our same gauges of success and achievement to determine our effectiveness with prayer. The purpose of prayer is not solely to get something or to make sure you do it right. It is to meet with God, and if you have done that, you have had a successful day in prayer.

You probably make your coffee, shower, work out, and read at similar times each day. That's because life itself naturally flows into rhythms, or you could even say habits. If these other things in our life naturally develop a rhythm, then so too should our prayer lives.

If you decide to go for a swim in the river, your first task is to get in the car, drive to the trail, and then find the river. Swimmers of all body types, skill sets, and SAT scores have all stood at the edge of this river. They can admire its beauty, feel the breeze, and imagine the refreshing nature of its flow. We can compare their strengths and weaknesses, but not a single one of them can swim without first making the jump.

You can tell yourself a million stories of why you shouldn't talk to God or that you're not doing it right. You can make excuses, and it's easy to find a list of them. I can't tell you exactly what a consistent prayer life will look like for you. We can, however, look at what currently is and state that as a fact. Is what you have been doing working? Do you feel empowered, at peace, and filled with hope? Have you found consistency in the midst of a chaotic life? If the answer is no, the only conclusion is that it's time for something new.

When moments of life happen, these rhythms naturally tend to kick in. It's the same trigger that would cause me to complain when someone gets on my nerves or to blame God when my family member is sick. Most rhythms you can start just like clicking play on Spotify. You can prepare your favorite chair by the natural light, make coffee, and pull out your journal. As much as I love preparation and planning, some rhythms just happen to you. You drive past an awful wreck and in an unexpected moment you have the choice to people-watch or to enter into prayer. When you hear those voices of doubt at work, you can let them sit or submit them to God. You can obsess over your child's health and safety, or you can submit them to God. I often find myself either complaining or praying, worrying or trusting—two different choices leading to two different outcomes.

Just like I had to listen for my song, you may have to wait on your rhythm. It won't come overnight, and it won't be easy. You will know when you find it and will notice it when it hits. Based on your personality, it could be at 5 a.m., your lunch break, or even 10 o'clock at night. God is much more interested in your commitment than your method. Give yourself permission to try new things. Most important, don't quit when you miss a day.

You may feel like an introvert, but there's a side of your spirit that wants to get out on the dance floor. Every part of your being wants to experience the joy and fullness of life in prayer. What are you waiting on? You're not that good at it anyway! You will never be perfect; that's why you are to focus your life on the One who is. Glance to the side, turn your ear up, find the rhythm, and simply jump into it.

"Are you tired? Worn out? Burned out on religion? Come to me. Get away with me and you'll recover your life. I'll show you how to take a real rest. Walk with me and work with me—watch how I do it. Learn the unforced rhythms of grace. I won't lay anything heavy or ill-fitting on you. Keep company with me and you'll learn to live freely and lightly."

Matthew 11:28-30

As much as I hate to break the rhythm of this carefully curated book, I couldn't help myself. I'm not a Bible commentator, but this verse has so much depth.

"Walk with me"
—*Don't feel any pressure.*

"Work with me"
—*I think you can do more than you think.*

"Watch how I do it"
—*I would never ask you to do something I don't do.*

This verse promises to lead us to rest, but it also leads us to a place of rest in prayer. First, as we tackle a deeper place of prayer and intimacy with God, He is with us. We have grown accustomed to one of our life's greatest needs being met on day one. We are all afraid deep down to be or die alone; God promises us that it isn't going to happen. Second, as we work on our new journey of prayer, we may work, but it will be alongside Him. Last and the most complex, we watch Him do it. Jesus is so kind that He wouldn't ask us to do something and then not leave an example. We can look to the Scriptures and recall all of the times Jesus prayed. We can look to the prayer book of the Bible: Psalms. That may not have been Jesus in the flesh but the Spirit praying through David and many others. This is how I would summarize this passage in "Jordan's translation":

Are you tired of feeling the way you do? Come hangout with me for a while! You will have to slow down, it won't be easy, but I'll teach you a new way. You've been carrying all of that heaviness but I'll teach you to lay it down. Until then, let me help you carry that!

Even when you don't feel Him,
He is still there.

You've been carrying around
weariness, but I'll teach you
to lay it down.

XI. ROOM

"There are some battles that can only be won in your prayer closet," I said to my friend after we discussed some slight tension in his relationship. We couldn't quite identify what was going on. After he shared, all I could feel was a heavy weight that wouldn't go away. There was nothing in the natural that we could identify. Without Christ, my best answer would have been to tell him to toughen up, be patient, or simply forget about it for a while.

In the moment, I felt prompted to remind him that some of our battles are not of this world. Strong men and women, particularly those raised in religion or with more childhood responsibility, may struggle here. As we age and experience life, the way to solve problems in our jobs, marriages, and personal lives is to act. Problem-solving is a top quality that companies look for when hiring new team members. So what do job interviews and skill sets have to do with our faith?

Prayer is spiritual problem-solving. The reason employers want problem-solvers is because there's sure to be plenty of them. To be good at your job, you have to be ready for whatever comes your way any given day.

My friend was recently planting a church in our city. He began to prepare his first email campaign and interest social meetings. After all, he knew that he couldn't plant a church in a new city by himself. He was called by God to shepherd the people and teach the Scriptures. Along with him were all of the people in our community called to ministry who would never be called "pastor."

A wise man in our church looked at my pastor friend and bluntly said to him, "Don't have anyone on your launch team who won't pray."

To take on a new city with a church plant, shouldn't we be looking for the best worship leaders, photographers, friendly greeters, and kids' ministry workers? Shouldn't each person line up so we can check for skinny jeans, tattoos, fat bank accounts, and fedoras?

If we believe the Bible, and we heed the advice of our fellow church member, we would still first look for those who pray. Someone once said that "the prayer room is the heartbeat of every church"—that life change, salvation, and loving others truly flow from and are sustained by the prayer room.

Can I take it a step further?

> The prayer room is the heartbeat of every family.

> The prayer room is the heartbeat of every business.

> The prayer room is the heartbeat of every marriage.

> The prayer room is the heartbeat of walking with Jesus.

I don't question for one moment our willingness to solve a problem. We'll quickly join the local nonprofit in driving a hammer and nail to build homes for the homeless. We'll tip extra at the restaurant. We'll send a Christmas box overseas at Christmas. But the question is, will we pray?

It has never been our willingness to solve a problem but our understanding in how to do so. Don't get me wrong, I'm not launching a campaign for complacency and laziness here. There are and will always be times when your hands and feet should go to work for the Lord. However, I am asking that the next time an issue or obstacle comes up, would you take a few moments before responding? Could the moments when we work our fingers to the bone, or worry ourselves to sleep, be more easily solved on our knees before bed?

This doesn't just work for solving problems. For if the foundation of our walk with Jesus is to solve problems, get blessings, or achieve religious tasks, we have missed the point. The prayer room is alive to connect our hearts to God. To solely focus on Jesus is the goal of prayer. God is everywhere, don't get me wrong. That doesn't mean we are always aware of it.

To avoid the prayer room as a believer is to skip the locker room before the game. To leave the kitchen when you want to cook. To turn the lights off when you want to see. You can still function and survive, but you're making it harder than it needs to be.

A room or specific place is not essential to our survival but it is encouraged. How many times have you heard someone tell a child, "You're really making this hard on yourself, aren't you?"

As believers, we unknowingly spend most of our time doing things *for* God instead of being with Him. Chapters and books have been written on this thought alone. The prayer room (or as your grandma would say, prayer closet) is simply about being *with* God. It is to solely bless Him and declare Him as holy above all things.

I want to offer a few practical thoughts here. You may wonder how this differs from your "place" with God that we mentioned earlier in the book. On our best days, the prayer room is where we go to solely focus on God. We step in because our soul beats to bless the Father. On other days, the prayer room can be entered because of a trigger. As I said, a problem or worry arises and that triggers our need for God, which reminds us that we need to pray. At the least, some of us just may feel "off" on a Tuesday afternoon.

I'd like to think that we're all super holy, that we wake up with four hours of intense prayer on the mountaintop. But most of us work 40 hours a week, and some of you have kids to feed and lunches to pack.

I *love* the idea of a space in your home to pray. I would also encourage you to find a house of prayer in your city, a room at a local church, a spot at the library or local park. When you have time, go, and do as much of that as you can.

But some days your prayer room may be that deep breath after the last kid gets out of the car for school. You may settle into the couch after your spouse leaves for work. You may get a few minutes at a coffee shop between meetings.

"Hey, God." You just entered a house of prayer.

One thing to remember is that you are the house of prayer He's hoping to dwell in. So much of God's plan for the world flows through you and through me. Because of Christ in us, we offer hope and extend grace to all around us. The world embracing a life of prayer depends on you and me living out what we wish others to be. It's less about a physical location and more about an atmosphere. Is God saying, "Come to Me, all of you, with all your things. I'm here to help"?

I believe He is.

Is He saying, "You are the house I want to dwell in, the living and breathing representation of Christ on Earth"?

He is.

Pause
Anytime
Anywhere

Deep breaths
Enter in

Bless the Lord
Day and night
Bless His holy name

The prayer room is the heartbeat

XII. WORD

We all have come from various backgrounds, experiences, and belief systems. If you grew up in a strict home, you may view God as a disciplinarian. If your parents were atheists, you may still be contemplating if God is real. Maybe you've lost a family member or friend, and you wonder if God is really who He says He is. How could God be good when all we see around us is conflict, lack, and struggle? Am I allowed to admit I don't know if anyone is actually listening to my prayers?

Our ability to commit to God naturally begins with how we truly view Him. We usually will not fully commit to something we're unsure of anywhere else in life. God may be a part of many people's lives, but He is everything to very few. The gospel points to one route in following Jesus: *Humbly die to yourself, and follow Me.*

Raising your hand in a church isn't enough; it is also the new life that begins when you walk out the back doors. This is the narrow road that very few will find. God is not selfish and begging for our attention. He is a gracious Father, giving us plenty of time and opportunity to choose His way. Why don't more people find it? Living in our minds are many half-truths about God and His ways. We view

Him most often through our own feelings, experiences, and emotions. This is not and will never be the biblical way to view God or ourselves. God may be invisible but He is very real. This is by no means a pharisaical cry to be perfect or to never love other things. It is the truth that God is to be the primary focus and direction of our lives—the sails on a windy day, a refreshing drink in the heat, an anchor in the storm. That's what our Father is to be to us.

It's not and will never be about pursuing Him perfectly. David was a man after God's own heart. He was king of Israel and a prophetic picture of the Messiah to come. Seems important, right? David sinned against God, hooked up with his neighbor, had her husband killed, and had a child with her. Wait, what? That's a man after God's own heart?

We have put aside perfection, so we can now take a deep breath. We can clearly see that David was a man after God's own heart not because of his perfection but because He was unwilling to give up! He relentlessly pursued knowing his Father more, no matter what was in his way.

Throughout Psalms we see every human emotion on display. David felt it all, but his deepest longing was to return to pursuing his God. As we come to know and believe God more, the aim is to relentlessly pursue and grow in our relationship with Him. The ball is in our court; God has already done His part.

The same concept of reciting or declaring your prayers can translate into how you deal with Scripture. On the days when you don't feel like praying, there is a likely chance you will not feel like studying the Word.

I want to be clear that I am not trying to coddle the next generation and have them never go to war with their feelings. There is very much a time and place for putting certain feelings to death. Within this context, we are comparing praying or not praying at all, spending time with God or moving on with our day.

In a way, practicing what this guide teaches is the start of going to war, squaring up against an enemy you are so used to bowing down to—your feelings. Slightly pushing past your feelings to prayer is the gateway to intimacy.

God will always honor any step that we make toward Him, big and small. It is the path of the righteous willing to move forward in uncertainty, hopelessness, and weakness. *I may be weak but I am also willing.*

As I began to work through my emotions in prayer, I felt like something was missing. If there is anything the devil could possibly hate more than you pushing forward in prayer, it's you reading and declaring the infallible Word of God over your life. I was struggling with anxiety and worry; even when I was praying I felt like something was missing. A friend texted me and reminded me that Jesus often declared the Word against the world: *The Word never bows to your weakness; it stands on its own, with or without you.*

The Word doesn't need our approval or endorsement to be true. The same concepts of planting, consistency, and rhythm can be applied to your time in the Word. The next step after hearing and declaring is obeying the Word. As I mentioned, we can claim the promises but many of the promises are tied to a command. Let's look at a few instances in which the Word can go to work for you.

Worry and Anxiety

> Don't worry about anything; instead, pray about
> everything. Tell God what you need, and thank him for
> all he has done. Then you will experience God's peace,
> which exceeds anything we can understand. His peace
> will guard your hearts and minds as you live in Christ
> Jesus.
> (Philippians 4:6-7)

Fear

> Such love has no fear, because perfect love expels all
> fear. If we are afraid, it is for fear of punishment, and this
> shows that we have not fully experienced his perfect love.
> (1 John 4:18)

Shame

> Weeping may last through the night, but joy comes with
> the morning. (Psalm 30:5b)

Doubt

> I pray that God, the source of hope, will fill you
> completely with joy and peace because you trust in him.
> Then you will overflow with confident hope through the
> power of the Holy Spirit. (Romans 15:13)

Sickness

> And the prayer offered in faith will make the sick person
> well; the Lord will raise them up. If they have sinned, they
> will be forgiven. (James 5:15)

Finances

> And this same God who takes care of me will supply all
> your needs from his glorious riches, which have been
> given to us in Christ Jesus. (Philippians 4:19)

Destiny and Dreams

> I gave you a land on which you had not labored, and
> cities which you had not built, and you have lived in
> them; you are eating of vineyards and olive groves which
> you did not plant. (Joshua 24:13)

Identity

> For we are God's masterpiece. He has created us anew
> in Christ Jesus, so we can do the good things he planned
> for us long ago. (Ephesians 2:10)

You won't find an issue that you're facing that the Word can't speak into. While Scripture can be used to offer encouragement, it can also help you fight. Jesus and the devil both practiced declaring the Word. In Matthew 11, Jesus went into the wilderness to fast for 40 days and nights. When He was approached by the devil, His response surprised me. The Son of God, equally a part of the Trinity, didn't even use human words to fight the devil. Three different times, Jesus responded to temptation with the Word:

> "If you are the Son of God, tell these stones to become loaves
> of bread."

But Jesus told him, "No! *The Scriptures say,*
'People do not live by bread alone,
   but by every word that comes from the mouth of God.'''

"If you are the Son of God, jump off! For the Scriptures say,'
   He will order his angels to protect you.
And they will hold you up with their hands
   so you won't even hurt your foot on a stone."

Jesus responded,
"*The Scriptures also say,*
'You must not test the Lord your God.'''

Next the devil took him to the peak of a very high mountain
   and showed him all the kingdoms of the world and their glory.
"I will give it all to you," he said,
"if you will kneel down and worship me." "

Get out of here, Satan," Jesus told him.
"*For the Scriptures say,*'
You must worship the Lord your God
   and serve only him.'''

And then the most comforting ending: "Then the devil went away."

We could speculate on the many reasons this happened, but fasting often causes us to be physically weak and spiritually strong. While Jesus' body was likely weak, His spirit was strong enough to know the perfect response to the devil's games.

When we as humans face moments of temptation, we're usually not thinking right. That's why it's so powerful to invite the unchanging Word of God into our atmosphere. You can be hopeless and still declare hope-filled verses. You can be sad and speak words of joy. Your situation doesn't have to be better and you don't even have to pretend. In your weakness, His Word is strong!

The good gifts are waiting,
the playbooks, blueprints, and the
glimmers of hope—not if you are good,
but if you simply choose to slow down
and open them.

Slightly pushing past your
feelings to prayer is the
gateway to intimacy

XIII. GOD

A healthy prayer life begins with an accurate view of God. For me, what has been the most beneficial is to put everything I believe about God on the table. If you grew up in the church, a lot of what you know will be true; but some of it will not. Pastors, leaders, and parents may have shown you an accurate view of God. Far too often, people in positions of power manipulate God's Word for their own agenda. They use Scripture to distort the gospel of love and grace.

By laying everything down, we say, "God, I don't want to know about You. I want to know You."

God is not a mean judge with a gavel waiting to banish you to hell. He is a loving Father, the perfect Shepherd, consistent and unchanging. He simply cannot resist answering with love and grace when you call. It's not just what He does; it's who He is.

So how do we gauge and comprehend a consistent God in a world where everyone has shifting opinions? Someone once said, "It is much more enjoyable to talk to God than to talk about Him." In reality, most of us have spent our lives talking or hearing *about* God. I went to a Christian college for a year. On any day, you could find students across the cafeteria debating topics and views about faith and God. What you'd find less of was people consistently sharing about being in love with Jesus.

There is no place that reveals God's heart like His Word. It is the first and only place we can go and trust that it's the foundation of who He is. Our lives, emotions, and relationships often do not show us who God is and who we are. Scripture is the mirror that reflects both, perfectly and completely. "In the beginning the Word already existed. The Word was with God, and the Word was God. The Word gave life to everything that was created, and his life brought light to everyone" (John 1:1-2,4).

Although I believe this book will speak to people in all walks of life. It will be most effective paired with a healthy diet in the Scriptures. That's one reason I wanted to include verses in each section. Don't stop there! In the spiritual realm, your appetite grows from eating and consuming the Word, not distancing from it. The more we taste, the more we enjoy. When we begin to realize the work that the Word is doing in us, it will then flow into our daily practices. "Your word is a lamp to guide my feet and a light for my path" (Psalm 119:105).

At one point in my life, I didn't read the Scriptures. I said, "I'm a Christian, and I love Jesus, but I don't like to read." But then I discovered that the more I was willing to read for five minutes at a time, the more I began to desire it. A pastor once said, "You know you are spiritually sick if you no longer desire worship and the Word."

There is no condemnation here. We all get a cough or a cold once in a while. Without proper rest, exercise, and nutrition, sickness can easily get worse.

If you don't want the Word, that probably just means that you forgot how good it tastes. For some of you, this looks like sitting down for ten minutes a day and being open to God and what He wants to show you. For others, God is calling you deeper, to unpack more, to discover hidden truths.

As you open the Scriptures, remember that you are not doing a chore; you are reading a love letter, written for you and for me. Humbly lay down all that you think God is and discover who He really is. The Word helps me see myself. It shows me who God really is, not just what people have told me about Him.

"All Scripture is inspired by God and is useful to teach us what is true and to make us realize what is wrong in our lives. It corrects us when we are wrong and teaches us to do what is right. God uses it to prepare and equip his people to do every good work."

2 Timothy 3:16-17

God already knows your needs,
but He still wants you to tell Him.

God, I don't want to
just know about you.

XIV. WANTS

I have often studied verses on prayer and wondered why the concepts and promises presented looked vastly different from most of what I had experienced.

> Ask for anything and it will be yours. (John 14:13)

> You will pray to him, and he will hear you, and you will fulfill your vows. (Job 22:27)

> Whatever you ask for in prayer, believe that you have received it, and it will be yours. (Mark 11:24)

I do believe in the power of prayer. But maybe some of these were taken out of context. right?! These are a bit too radical for me. There is no way I can fully accept a verse about asking for anything. After all, many of us have only prayed "Your will be done" our entire life.

If we are willing to be honest, many of us have have prayed for things that did not come to pass. In life, our prayers are often tossed up in a random act of desperation. Maybe if I talk to God and say "in Jesus' name," things will get better. Some even have the belief that "I dare not ask God for what I want specifically though." The thought that we, empowered by the Spirit, can ask for anything sounds too much for me.

Man-made religion consistently breeds timidity. Unhealthy leaders hide behind titles and hold to authority that they created for themselves. "Come to us. We'll pray for you and as you. We'll teach you the Word. Don't worry about learning to do it yourself."

A healthy and reverent fear of God has gone too far. Many raised in traditional religious environments slowly distance themselves from the great Oz-like God of their religion. Our interactions with self-centered parents or leaders unknowingly reflected onto our view of God. God may care about me but only with His motives and needs front and center. It seems we have drifted far from "approaching the throne of grace with confidence." (More on this in the next chapter.)

I have discovered something this past year: the Bible is radical. To assume otherwise is to dilute the Scriptures that many across the world have risked their lives for. If you actually read the Scriptures line by line, believe it, and proclaim it to others, people will start to look at you funny (even Christians).

On that hillside near Galilee, Jesus' disciples kept letting Him know that it was late and everyone was getting hungry. There were somewhere around 20,000 people (men, women, and children) listening to Jesus teach that day. Many hours had passed as people sat and listened. The disciples were letting Jesus know loud and clear what the people wanted: They wanted to be fed and some of them wanted it now.

We do the very same thing in our prayer life. We pray when we want things and neglect it when we don't. I don't have any objections to you making your request known. In fact, I believe it's one of the foundations of a healthy prayer life. I would like to propose something though that might increase your rate of answered prayers. When we pray on our own authority and desires, we will have hits and misses. We are praying from our own experience, heart, and circumstances. This is nothing to feel guilty about; we are human and often doing the best we can.

When we instead humbly submit and pray, empowered by the Spirit, our hearts start to look a lot more like His. We begin to pray like He would.

When Jesus was on the hillside, He gave the people what they wanted (food), so He could feed them what they really needed (spiritual food). Jesus met their need with a miraculous moment of feeding everyone. Their stomachs may have been grumbling to eat, but many of their souls had been starving for quite some time. God met their physical need; now He could continue to work on the inside. They were ready to get to their Sunday lunch even though the Word was still being preached. (Some things don't change even after thousands of years.) If they were worried about food, we have to conclude that they were unaware of the moment they were in. They didn't comprehend who they were sitting under. The Son of God was teaching in their midst.

Could it be that some of our prayers fall short not because of God but because of us? Could we struggle with prayer not because we're lazy but because we are unaware of the moment we're in?

We so easily forget what we have and who we have access to. For some of us, we simply don't believe God will give us what we ask. At the root, we don't trust our wants because we don't trust ourselves.

The great God of heaven and Earth can give you everything you will ever need and still not give you what you want. Suppose Jesus had ignored their request for food. He would have still been giving them what they needed while ignoring what they wanted. They wanted food, but they needed a reviving message, the word and breath of God.

I have fumbled around in religious practices trying to do the right thing for quite some time. This only left me frustrated and constantly focused on my shortcomings instead of on Christ. Now the focus of my entire life is to follow Jesus and become more like Him. The more I become like Jesus, the more my wants in prayer look less like me and more like Him. When you pray with the heart of Christ, you no longer are tossing up thoughts to heaven. Through Jesus, you are humbly approaching God with all of the scriptures behind you.

We can all feel a little more boldness rising. I think we often forget about the boy who gave up his five loaves and two fish. Wasn't he hungry? Didn't he want to eat what his parents had prepared for him?

Prayer is often about giving up more than it is about getting. The more I lay down, the more I can pick up. I pray for what I want, and I get what I need. This reaches its most difficult climax when what we "need" is to wait. I'm sure his lunch would have tasted good. I bet his mom could cook a mean fried fish. Maybe he just thought, *I'm not sure who this man is, but I feel the power in his teachings. He wants what I have, and he can have it. He can have the lunch that's in my hands today.*

I can promise you that a full belly didn't compare to watching his lunch multiply in their hands. Seeing the other people eat and experiencing this unbelievable moment, he waited and ended up with food and so much more.

Prayer is about doing our part on the front end, then trusting God with the other side! I pray to have the childlike faith of this boy, willing to give up what's in my hand for God's greater plan.

A few months ago I was preparing for my first trip to Africa. I had been asked to tag along and film for a nonprofit. It was a last-minute trip and it would only be my friend Daniel and me. As I began to think about the trip, my emotions overwhelmed me with the idea of how many hurting people we'd encounter. In the middle of a global pandemic, the slums of Kenya had to be worse off than before.

I sat on my comfortable bed and asked God, "If You can do these amazing miracles, why can't You do them through me?" My reasoning was a bit selfish, but I thought, *If I'm going to uproot my life for a week, travel across the world in a pandemic, and cancel other paying jobs, what are You going to do, God? These people are desperate and I'm going to be claiming to represent You.* I quietly and humbly began to pray that I would see miraculous signs and wonders—truly for the people we would encounter and not for myself. I had been on other missions trips but never once had I prayed a prayer like this. I imagined all that could happen, the crowds of people all coming to be filled with the Spirit!

When we finally landed in Kenya, this prayer stayed near to my heart. As I thought about all of the hurting people, I asked for God to heal them. We spent a few days with a host family, filmed our project, and had one more day to spare. Nothing "crazy" was happening, but I felt so much peace in my first visit there. The people's hospitality, kindness, and joy were overwhelming.

For most of the trip we stayed near the city, but one day we loaded up our car to take medical supplies to a hospital. Afterward, we would go straight to the airport. A part of me started to think about the miracles I had hoped to see on this trip, the countless lives giving themselves to Jesus. From the physical eye, we just hadn't seen what I was believing for. During a global pandemic, with restaurants and public areas closed, this trip just looked different.

After more than two hours in the car, we were driving on dirt roads in the middle of nowhere. We pulled into the hospital, which was no bigger than a school cafeteria. The police chief, the elder of the city, and the owner of the hospital all awaited us as if we were dignitaries or doctors. "We'll give you the grand tour," they said.

As we followed the gentlemen, I stayed in a posture of prayer. We passed a door on which was scribbled with a red marker "AIDS testing here." He pointed to the door and said just that. He pointed to another door, where a family was sitting, and said, "Then that's the room you go in if you may be positive." *Um… did he really just call them out?* I thought.

I guess it was so common for someone to be sitting in front of that door that he didn't think anything of it. I had left my attitude of prayer and continued to observe the space, reassuring everyone

I was a college dropout and not a doctor. I passed the family in front of the door and this thought came to my mind: *Lay hands on that boy.*

Wait, what? That couldn't have been the Holy Spirit. He speaks to me, but touching that boy made no sense. I rationalized in my mind that there are cultural practices and you don't just walk up to a woman and her kids and pray for them. We made our way outside and I had that sinking feeling that I had missed an opportunity. *God, were You really trying to work through me, and I missed the opportunity?* We ended up on the other side of the property and I honestly was considering leaving our group to go back inside. But then I saw a boy popping his head through the bushes. He had followed us the rest of the way.

I walked over to him and asked him how he was. I began to pray under my breath and I put my hand on his shoulder. I asked God to impart to him whatever he needed. I asked the boy what his name was. I didn't make a scene and that boy never knew I was praying. I'm not exactly sure what happened, but something deep in my spirit tells me that God gave him whatever he needed that day. He could have done it without me, but He chose to do it through me. Praise God! If I want to really speak in faith, I pray that the Spirit traveled to his family too, because God is just that good.

So, what are we to make of this story and my trip to Kenya? I learned a very important lesson on faith and prayer. God will never punish us for setting the bar too high. I spoke and believed for countless signs and wonders—not for myself but for all of the broken and hurting people suffering during a pandemic. In all reality, I saw only a few interactions.

I shot for the stars, and God is sovereign in the end. God could have done more, but it wasn't because of my lack of faith. We must trust Him on the back end of our bold and faith-filled prayers. To say that what happened in and around me wasn't significant would be to tell God that He doesn't know what He's doing.

The Demons' Request:

We see in Scripture Jesus confronting a demon-possessed man. The demons knew they had no choice but to leave the man they were in. They could not compete with Jesus. "Jesus, right before you cast us out, would you mind not making us leave the region. Can you just put us in those pigs over there?"

To the people who believe we should not ask God for anything, I kindly disagree. You mean to tell me a demon can make requests and we as children of God can't? I don't say this lightly, but if I can't pray to God, if I can't tell Him what I need, then I don't want to be here! It is one of the true hopes of my existence—His presence and His help. I need it daily.

Just like the boy with his lunch, he had no idea what would come from his open-handed gesture—his willingness to trust God. This historically accurate story that has lasted thousands of years was all dependent upon a boy being willing to give up what he wanted. You see, prayer doesn't get rid of our troubles, sickness, and struggles; it places them in God's hands.

When we lay down our wants in prayer, the impossible doesn't just become possible; it is now probable. It is radical.

It is Jesus.

"And my God will supply every need of yours according to his riches in glory in Christ Jesus"

Philippians 4:19

"God is more eager to answer than we are to ask."

—Smith Wigglesworth

I pray for what I want,
and I get what I need.

XV. GOOD

Are you good?

It's a slightly different question than "How are you?" Is it implying that you are or aren't good? I guess that would depend on the context. If you have ever been asked this, you were answering a question framed for a moment of time.

Today as I ask this question, I am not merely speaking of your feelings today, but I want you to imagine that you're standing at the end of your life. Are you good?

> "Well, I'm a good person, I think."

> "I have done more good than bad."

> "I have trusted God and loved my neighbor."

Through and through, are you good?

> "Well, I guess not, because there are parts of me that aren't always right."

Great. Now we can get to work.

I have no idea your religious background or upbringing, but if you were involved in organized religion, you were probably told that you needed to be good. Whether you're a Christian or not, I need to tell you something that you are aware of; you just may not have heard someone say it to you: *You are not good.* I love you enough to tell you that this is certainly the case. Don't worry. I've had to get off my high horse many times in life.

As a young believer, I had the "us and them" mentality. We are Christians; they are the lost. We are over here because we do right; they are over there because they do wrong. After a season of running from God, I was humbled and reminded that there is no us and them. There is just us and then there's Jesus.

I realized how wrong things can go for me and through me when I attempt to remove Jesus from my daily life. I have studied a fair amount on Hitler, the Jews, and the horrific events of the Holocaust. I think when we look back at this time in history, we have rationalized that Hitler and the Nazis could do something like that. Let me simplify it for you: humans did that. The similarity between you, me, and Hitler is that we are humans. Humans left to themselves are capable of killing six million innocent men, women, and children.

The feeling of waking up every morning needing to be good enough is exhausting. I have stayed in sin cycles for years too long simply because I was trying to be strong enough. I was trying to fight my battles and then asking God to bless them.

We are not superior to anyone. Much of the teaching throughout

Scripture reminds us that we are not in an exclusive club. Jesus said, "Come to Me, *all.*" I started living a new life when I realized two things: I'm not strong enough and I don't trust myself. Oh how Jesus delights in us finally admitting the truth. If I'm not strong enough, then I need someone to be strong for me. If I don't trust myself, then I need someone trustworthy.

Prayer positions us to receive God's goodness.

> Confess your sins to each other and pray for each other so that you may be healed. The earnest prayer of a righteous person has great power and produces wonderful results. Elijah was as human as we are, and yet when he prayed earnestly that no rain would fall, none fell for three and a half years! Then, when he prayed again, the sky sent down rain and the earth began to yield its crops.
> (James 5:16-18)

Prayer and confession together are healing for the body and soul. We need God but we also need each other. Humans, filled with the Spirit, are the physical representation of Christ on the earth.

We seek individually but we also grow together. I must warn you, a soft rebuke is coming for most of us here. Many people desire to walk with and help others in their life. Oftentimes this leads to us listening to them, genuinely caring, and then offering our lengthy advice. We listen a lot, and we talk even more. James says, "Confess your sins to each other and pray."

Healthy accountability is confession and prayer, not confession and advice. I am not saying we can never talk or give advice. We just all show by our actions that we value our talking more than our prayers. We are putting a stake in the ground and believing that we can help people with our words more than our pleas to the throne of grace. May we all repent with this new knowledge and return to the biblical view of accountability. Prayer is a way that we can impart the goodness of God to those around us. Confession and prayer— whatever follows is useful but not without the foundation of prayer.

We often see a focus on getting our heart right before we pray. Are we capable of doing anything with our own heart? Every sin and shortcoming are heart issues. If all of our problems flow from the heart, our inability to cure our own diseases can cause a sense of fear and disappointment. Psalms gives us a picture of what we're to do with our heart and spirit. Simply submit them to God, the healer and redeemer.

"Create in me a clean heart, O God. Renew a loyal spirit within me" (Psalm 51:10).

In James, we see that Elijah was fully human, yet when he prayed that it wouldn't rain, it didn't. The whole earth responded to Elijah's bold prayers, yet many of us don't believe simple prayers can change our own life. It took me 27 years to admit this, "God, without You, there is nothing good in me. On my own I can do very little." The beauty of this harsh reality is that *with* Him, there is nothing we can't become or accomplish.

I studied the word "righteousness" pretty intently over the past year, mainly because I heard a lot of people saying it and I didn't understand it. Another way I like to say it is right-ness. Before diving deeper, I would have told you the Christian life is about pursuing righteousness. Where I veered a little off was the belief that it was about being right. I think it took failure after failure for me to finally say, "God, there is nothing right in me. I am a sinner. I am wicked and capable of anything if You're not with me." This is not self-shaming; it's simply saying that whatever is right with me is not good enough.

If you have broken any law, that makes you a law breaker, not worthy of eternity in heaven. The pursuit of righteousness is essential to every believer. Paul said to live as if you're to be judged by the law! The difference in thinking is that the pursuit is *His* righteousness.

The more I studied Scripture, the more I realized that most of the Bible talks less about our righteousness and more about His.

> He is good.
> He is right.
> Without Him, we are not.

> "Because Abraham believed God's words, his faith transferred God's righteousness into his account" (Romans 4:3).

At first it seems a little discouraging, but that's before we mention that as believers, *all* of Him is available to us. *All.*

My life changed when I woke up and stopped trying to be good enough. I pray, "God, I lay down whatever is good in me and I pick up everything that's right with You. Clothe me with Your righteousness. Be the goodness in and through me."

It is God's righteousness made visible through the faithfulness of Jesus Christ. And now all who believe in him receive that gift. For there is really no difference between us, for we all have sinned and are in need of the glory of God. Yet through his powerful declaration of acquittal, God freely gives away his righteousness. His gift of love and favor now cascades over us, all because Jesus, the Anointed One, has liberated us from the guilt, punishment, and power of sin!

Romans 3:21-24

I'm not strong enough.

I don't trust myself.

I'm not good.

He is strong enough.

He is trustworthy.

He is good.

Prayer positions us to
receive God's goodness.

XVI. FIGHT

You and I both wake up every morning, pull the covers off, and let our feet hit the ground. At this moment, every single one of us is still human. No matter how much we pray, worship, or behave right, as long as we are here on Earth, we will be human. Man-made religion has made people feel like they can no longer be human. As believers, the reality of our current humanity does not mean we are not becoming something more. Sometimes I wonder if God is more accepting of our humanity than we are. Understanding our human nature will release a flow of grace and patience as we continue to pursue the things of God.

I attended a nondenominational and Pentecostal church growing up. This was a fruitful house to grow up in. I learned to dwell in God's presence, hear from the Holy Spirit, and flow in the anointing. The negative side to the Spirit-filled movement is that at times we can mistakenly find ourselves chasing a moment or a feeling instead of Jesus. We can try to create something for ourselves instead of giving Him all of our attention. There is nothing wrong with the spontaneous, as long as it's in and through Him.

Most of us have experienced an unexpected and spontaneous

moment with God at least once. It's simply who He is. We just happened to "randomly" meet the person who led to the job. We got that check in the mail just in time. The doctor couldn't explain where your friend's sickness went. A life with Jesus is a life of spontaneous adventure.

You don't have to feel bad for starting your day with a set plan or prayer routine. This simply gets you into a flow. Every moment with God, each conversation and time you encounter Him, there is an opportunity for a complete turnaround. It is a time when every wrong thing can be made right. God is patient, and He often will work on us in parts and in seasons. He isn't trying to fix or change us all at once, even though we get that vibe from Christians more than we'd like. There is a reason Jesus asked, "Do you want to be healed?" in moments of healing in the Scriptures. When He touched them, they could not remain the same. The lesser power must bow to the greater one. The King had power over the things that had attached themselves to His people.

Just because we *are* human, however, doesn't mean we have to fight our own earthly battles. If I run at my problems or temptations alone, they are going to sucker punch me to the ground sooner or later. One of my favorite boxers is Ryan Garcia. When I see his training videos on Instagram, he honestly doesn't look that powerful because he's moving his hands so fast—right then left, his hands moving so quickly against the punching bag. When you watch him in the ring, you'll see his left hook, and before your eyes can catch up, the other guy is flat on his back.

With God, you don't have to act all tough, big, and strong to defeat your opponent. You don't have to break walls, scream, or build up your muscles. You just need one hit, and that hit is *His* power, not yours. When you're working your practices and rhythms, you may not look that impressive. Sometimes you're just reading, praying, and sitting silently. It may even feel like life is passing you by while the world is clawing for success and external achievement. When you sit down each day, you are inviting God not only to be with you but also to work with you. You may not notice the difference each day, but when moments of insecurity, offense, or temptation come, you'll be prepared to enter the fight.

God is not slow; He is the creator of time, on time and quicker than light. Just because God isn't working on our time doesn't mean He's late. I can hear people asking, "If God isn't slow, then why am I waiting?" If you're waiting, then God has yet to decide to move. There may be obstacles around you, but they are not in His way; when He moves, nothing will stop His plan.

I'm afraid that when we fight our own battles, we look like a fool trying to wrestle in a boxing match—big red boxing gloves, like crabs crawling around on the ground. You are putting in great effort; you're just playing the wrong way. To raise a family, build a career, and acquire things, we can easily do this on our own. We are playing the world's game and submitting to earthly systems. Without God, we may very well have a "good life."

So much changes when we decide to pursue God. All of our goals are no longer pointed to this life but to the next. We set our sights on the heavenly city, the place where we will be forever. A commentary I once read said, "Life is just an internship for a heavenly assignment"; I felt so much peace in that line. The tension comes when we realize this is our temporary home. Everything must now be examined through this mindset.

We were using our own strength to build our earthly lives, now we attempt to use that same strength in our spiritual ones. Stepping into the spiritual ring is a different game; it's God's place, not ours. We can't continue to fight the old way. A pastor once said, "You can't win spiritual battles with earthly wisdom." If you're a "doer" like me, it's going to be very difficult for you to learn to yield to the Spirit's work—to humbly pause, pray, and declare the Word over your situations. In fact, it may even be the last thing you want to do. Believe it or not, prayer is a weapon of war.

"Keep watch and pray, so that you will not give in to temptation. For the spirit is willing, but the body is weak!" (Matthew 26:41, NLT). If we were fighting an earthly battle, yes, I'll take three AK 47s, please. But we are not. Your extra gym workouts, growing bank account, and self-defense courses will not help you fight the powers of darkness waging war against your home and your family.

Imagine that you receive a letter in the mail advertising the biggest fight night in history. Ten million dollars are on the line and your face is on the front cover of the flier. The one catch is that you can either fight yourself or trade places with a person of your choosing. Because of what is on the line, and your understanding of your fighting skills, you will probably give a professional fighter a call. No one will call you weak; they will say you're wise. You won't feel self-doubt and shame for weeks after your decision. The lesser power submits to the greater one.

Stand to your feet and square up, with prayer and the Word, because when God hits, He hits fast and He doesn't miss. You'll think to yourself, *How did I resist that? How did I keep the faith and not give up? How did I overcome my anxiety? How did I have the faith to give generously?* The answer is, you didn't; He did.

We have our part: we must call. We must seek and ask, but when we do, He answers and He comes.

Lauren Daigle's words in her song "Rescue" are so comforting:

> I will send out an army to find you
> In the middle of the darkest night
> It's true, I will rescue you
> I will never stop marching to reach you
> In the middle of the hardest fight
> It's true, I will rescue you
> I hear the whisper underneath your breath
> I hear you whisper, you have nothing left

My grandpa was always at my basketball games. He took me to car shows and was like a father figure to me. I wanted to make him proud and I desired his approval. Soon after he helped me buy my first car, he was diagnosed with pancreatic cancer. He went from running his business and attending all of my games to being speechless in a wheelchair. This larger-than-life figure in my life was now withering away by the day.

This may be the most difficult and helpless moment in prayer. *God, I have nothing left.* When he finally passed away of cancer, I had reached one of these moments. I left his house in my old Mazda 626. I quietly drove through the fields and farmland near his home.

I thought, *I have cried every tear. I have prayed every prayer for healing, which didn't come, and I am just existing. I don't have anything to give or anything to say and I don't feel much either.*

This may be one of the moments in prayer when you don't have to say a word. You just look to Him, and He looks back at you. He gives you what you need even when you don't know how to ask for it.

Jesus is the deliverer. He's the healer, but He is also a comforter. When I don't hear back in time, when I start to see things as hopeless, I look to Him, I admire all He has created, and I thank Him for all He has done. When you're tired of losing battles, you reach the point of surrender. This is the opportunity to put down your weapon and pick up your faith.

"You shall not fear them, for it is the Lord your God who fights for you"

Deuteronomy 3:22

Understanding our human nature will
release a flow of grace and patience as
we continue to pursue the things of God.

A life with Jesus is a life
of spontaneous adventure

XVII. PLANTING

I wish I could tell you that I have some illustrious garden overtaking my backyard, that I just picked some fresh veggies and the carrots are now sautéing in a pan. Sadly, that is not the case. I have always loved the idea of having a garden and I hopefully will have one in the near future. I want you to think of a gardener in your life, not just your dad's tomato plant but I mean someone with an actual garden that they have to take care of multiple times a week—that person who, when you pull into their driveway, looks up at you with a handful of weeds as if time was standing still. I hate to generalize or assume, but I'd be willing to bet that this gardener in your life is somewhat peaceful, welcoming, and maybe even quiet.

There is a skill set and patience that come with gardening; some call it a green thumb. I've unintentionally killed two fig trees in my life, which does threaten my hipster credentials. (I overwatered them, I under-watered them, then they died.) Although there is a skill set to gardening, there is also an equally important mindset. If you spend all weekend planting the garden with the wrong mindset, you'll wake up to dirt on Monday morning ready to destroy it in frustration. "*Where are all my plants?!*" you scream in a rage. You planted all the seeds, but you just didn't understand that it may be weeks or months before you see any plants break through.

If you saw a man destroying the garden he just planted the day before, you'd say he was a lunatic. As ridiculous as this sounds, we do it with our prayer lives every day. We pray, we pray, and we pray and nothing happens. We wake up on Monday morning after sending up those weekend prayers and toss our prayer journal because nothing happened.

The primary reason your prayer life is frustrating is because you have yet to realize that you're planting. If you are receiving nothing today, you must ask yourself this hard question: *Did I adequately plant (or pray) in the last season?* Ecclesiastes 11:6 says to plant your seed in the morning and keep busy all afternoon, for you don't know if profit will come from one activity or another—or maybe both.

Don't get me wrong, God can be instant and He will be. It's when we always expect Him to be that causes the most tension in our relationship with Him. This is hard. I'm not going to pretend like it's not. We do not get the luxury of praying without faith. You don't get so good at prayer that you no longer need to believe in God. You do not get to approach the throne of grace without Jesus. Our great High Priest is the one who makes us holy and clean.

> "So then, since we have a great High Priest who has entered heaven, Jesus the Son of God, let us hold firmly to what we believe. This High Priest of ours understands our weaknesses, for he faced all of the same testings we do, yet he did not sin. So let us come boldly to the throne

of our gracious God. There we will receive his mercy,
and we will find grace to help us when we need it most"
(Hebrews 4:14-16).

The unknown and uncertain steps in our journey of faith don't ever go away on this side of heaven. God is not trying to delegate prayer to us and leave the room; He's around to help for good. Scripture says that Jesus lives to intercede for us. What amazing news! Even when we don't feel like praying, Jesus is planting prayers for us at the throne of grace! I love in Ecclesiastes 11:6 when it says, "Plant your seed in the morning and keep busy all afternoon." This tells me to plant my prayers and then get back to working with God. Although I admire the monk lifestyle, we can't all spend our lives in a cell praying.

Here is more encouragement amidst the uncertainty: What God is growing in and around you can't be grown in a day.

I used to become quite frustrated when praying for other people in my life. Why weren't they changing? I took them to coffee, invited them to dinner, and bought them that trendy devotional. By my calculations they should have stopped overly drinking and cussing by now. As people continued to stay the same, I became more frustrated. I eventually prayed for God to show me His heart for them. I stopped complaining about them and started praying for them. It is easy to look at our immediate circumstances and surroundings to determine if we're praying right.

Sadly, man-made religion has made us question the power of our own faith if we see lack in the people around us. Would we say that

Jesus had no faith because the people around Him were so dirty? Of course not!

Good gardeners don't just plant seeds; they also care for them. Caring for your prayers is allowing them to change and grow at their pace—maybe even writing them down and returning to them when you begin to lose faith. Loving your friends is walking with them as they learn to follow Jesus. Gardeners don't stop looking over the dirt just because the plants aren't visible yet. They patiently wait, trusting in the work they've put in, and that nature will water the ground and cultivate the atmosphere for things to grow.

God, give me a heavenly perspective for the people and opportunities around me! Help me to look at the dirt and see the illustrious garden that's coming!

Our main frustration is usually with our most urgent prayers. I don't pray to become more humble and then cry when it hasn't happened yet. I pray for my sick grandpa and he passes away. I cry out for financial breakthrough and all I see are bills. I intercede for my child and they still won't listen. These are the moments when we truly want to throw our prayer journals out the window. We are not imposing on God that He should answer every prayer today. We do however push the things we deem to be urgent on Him and then distance from Him when they don't happen—God, did You miss my urgency on that one? I paid extra for overnight shipping! Jesus, if You had been here sooner, Lazarus would not have died.

I cannot tell you why every prayer is not answered. I can tell you time and time again, I've realized that God sees the span of my whole life and I'm just looking out a window. I am often only seeing one little part. I can't see the whole story, but He can. I know where I am, but He knows where I'm going.

I was in a season of working for myself and working from home. I had so much more time to get things done and work on my writing. Unfortunately, I was bad at managing my time and I started to get complacent with my lifestyle. The comfort I felt kept me from pursuing my writing and YouTube channel like I should have been. I prayed so often for God to give me motivation again, to help me figure out what was wrong. Shortly after, God seemed to be pushing me toward applying for a full-time job. This was the last thing I wanted as no one valued having their own schedule and freedom as much as I did. After all, I can write and pursue more of my personal stuff without a full-time job. I for some reason decided to take the job. It was hard, the adjustment took some time, but the more I worked the new job the more I realized what was happening.

My original goal and prayer were to be more motivated and disciplined toward my writing and videos. I thought I knew what had to happen for this to change. God would just magically wave His wand and all of these things would come into place. I've learned something about Him: when He wants to change us, He often changes our surroundings. He allows things in and around our lives to grow and develop us. He puts us in the most unlikely of places in some seasons. Could it be that you've been placed here for a specific purpose? As you try to work your way out, God is creating space for you to stay and grow. "It's not important who does the planting, or who does the watering. What's important is that God makes the seed grow" (1 Corinthians 3:7).

I thought the best thing for my life was to stay home and work for myself. I knew what I wanted, but God knew what I needed. Taking a full-time job in another city while I had a lot to do seemed like the wrong move. Planting our prayers and trusting God often don't seem like the right way either. Rest assured, He knows exactly what you need, right when you need it! We may be planting, but He is bringing the supernatural growth!

Eugene Peterson says, "Prayer is the disciplined refusal to act before God acts." You look like a crazy person to your friends when you're waiting and the world is going! There are times when I have had to lay worry and fear on the altar—when I put my stake in the ground and said, "God, You are in control. You are working this out for my good! I give You control."

Have you ever wondered what childlike faith looks like in an adult? You would look like a full-on crazy person!

How did a child react to this pandemic?
My dad's keeping me safe.

How does a child react when their parents are facing financial trouble?
My dad is going to work it out.

How does a child react when they keep messing up the same stuff?
My dad can teach me how to do better.

How does a child react when a problem shows up at the front door of their home?
My dad is handling it.

How does a child act when the bill comes to the dinner table?
My dad is paying.

If you're an adult who reacts like a child, you are probably the lunatic on the block—the crazy man living in the tree trunk and playing his ukulele. Operating with childlike faith is an invitation to the greatest trust fall. You are now daily feasting on the Lord's provision. Your eyes are set on the heavenly city and you are not moved by man. You have stepped into the frequencies of heaven. You are not just praying like God; you are praying with Him!

Lord, give us the faith of a child!

Someone once said that you live life forward but you understand it backward. Stop trying to understand why the weeds are back and just pick them. Stop beating yourself up because the tomatoes didn't survive but the fruit tree thrived. Just pick some fruit and rest in the fact that our job is to consistently plant. You are a gardener, so prepare the ground, plant, and wait. We are to sow seeds in faith and then let God do what He does best: bring the whole thing together.

"I tell you the truth, anyone who doesn't receive the Kingdom of God like a child will never enter it"

Luke 18:17

If God doesn't answer my prayer today, He is still good.

God, You are in control.

You are working this out for my good!

XVIII. ASSURANCES

I can see the cheesy infomercial now: "Purchase today, satisfaction guaranteed. This product is sure to revolutionize your life at midnight." After your four payments of $49.99, you find out if the item was all it was hyped up to be.

The world is really really good at making things look better than they are. With a background in photography, my job was to walk into a room or a space and make it look better than it was—rearranging furniture, closing windows, turning off lamps, and finding the perfect angle for the shot. Our social media feeds are all filled with moments that shine with perfect beauty and promise.

I want to present a thought that most of us have not thought of: "I love God, and I really do believe I'm a Christian, but what assurances do I have as I pray? Is there a satisfaction-guaranteed sticker on my prayer journal?"

I know that many of you are more spiritual than me. Up on your high horses you'll conquer the mountains of prayer without any guarantees. For me though, in my moments of weakness and vulnerability, I wonder what I can even count on. Is prayer just another thing that will hype me up and let me down?

Even with assurances, I do believe there's still room for faith and stepping into the unknown in our prayer lives. With that in mind, what are the things we can always hold to?

Although there are more, here are three truths I carry with me as I pray. They meet my human needs as I step out in faith.

1. He hears me.

Have you ever been halfway through venting to a friend and think to yourself, *Oh no, I'm doing it again.* You could even be typing a social media caption that sounds more like a counseling session. I think this flows from our deepest human need to be heard. While some of us are venting, others of us are suppressing. We're packing in our feelings and emotions tighter and tighter, spending day and night overthinking them or avoiding them altogether. For me, if I don't feel heard by God, I don't treat myself or others well. "And this is the confidence that we have toward him, that if we ask anything according to his will he hears us" (1 John 5:14).

We can't always rest in an exact response from God. We can however know that whatever we bring to Him, it will not get lost in the spam folder. He will read it and respond in the way that is best for us as His son or daughter.

As we release our thoughts and feelings to Him, we can trust that He not only hears but that He does so from a place of deep and intimate love.

2. He sees me.

I think that the only desire I have more than being heard is to be seen. "Okay, okay, I know you're listening, but do You see what I'm dealing with here, God? I understand the Scriptures, but I feel like I'm all alone here!"

Some of us may even feel like a young child crying, "Look at me, Dad! Look at me!" I probably told my parents to look at me more than any of my other siblings. I'd perform little shows in our living room and drag everyone to the couches to watch me. There is something so exhilarating about being in the spotlight.

In some ways, many of us desire to be seen because we had moments in our lives when we felt overlooked. There may have also been times when we put ourselves out there and faced rejection. The moment I'm asked to be in a group photo, I'm the first person I look at when I see it afterward. After all, I have to see how bad I look.

God is everywhere, He sees it all, yet He still keeps an eye on me. When I avoid the mirror, He doesn't get tired of looking at me. Whether I'm running a victory lap on my best day or stuck in bed feeling down, He hears me and He sees me.

I am so grateful that God looks at those the world overlooks. Not only that, but He sees our potential and even speaks into it. We can rejoice because we are fully seen by our loving father. "The lord is watching everywhere, keeping his eye on both the evil and the good" (Proverbs 15:3).

3. He knows me.

Before God created us, He knew us. If that doesn't take our breath away, I'm afraid we've grown accustomed to this beautiful reality.

God told the prophet Jeremiah, "I knew you before I formed you in your mother's womb"—*before you were born, I set you apart. I placed you exactly where I wanted you.* He knew us not because of anything we had done but because we were His.

In most relationships, we sit back and decide at which level we want to let people in. If they know about my thriving career, they'll be impressed. If they find out about my struggling marriage, they'll judge me.

Whether we like it or not, the call to follow Jesus includes the truth of being fully known by our Father. I believe the core of our ability to trust being known is found at the cross. Jesus took on the sins of the world, experiencing all, for you and for me. Depression, anxiety, pride, fear, rejection, and shame—He experienced them all on the cross at the fullest extent.

He's not sympathizing with us from a place of superiority but from a position of knowing exactly what we're dealing with.

Completeness

These three truths all flowed from the realization that if I started my day with Him, so many things would be different. If I leave my morning feeling seen, heard, and known by God, I need for nothing. I can now freely give to others and at times receive unexpected blessings from my Father.

So as we pray, what do we step into as we live from these three realities? Rest. Rest is our response to these assurances of the faith. Because of Christ, the One who intercedes on our behalf, we can rest. If we were praying on our own authority, we'd have to work. We'd have to till the ground and analyze our progress daily. Because of the Father's attention and embrace, we want for nothing.

The lord is my shepherd; I have all that I need.

He lets me rest in green meadows;

he leads me beside peaceful streams.

He renews my strength.

He guides me along right paths,

Bringing honor to his name.

Psalm 23:1-3

God, I'm thankful that You see me, You hear me, and You know me. I rest today in the finished work of the cross.

It's ok to rest

XIX. CONVERSATION

If friendship is a two-way street, then so too is talking to God. It is much easier to believe that I can just sit under the shade tree and wait for God to speak, that my contribution as a mere human is to wait and do only when God says to. There is a beautiful reality to this New Testament prayer life: it's that God not only wants to talk to us; He also wants us to talk to Him.

"Jordan, I get it. I think we learned that in the basics of Christianity."

Okay, well, how much do you do it? I find that I judge my level of belief based not on what I know but on how I act. I didn't set out on this project to teach you the perfect way to pray. I set out to give you a framework. This framework then leads to only you and God, a place I can never go with you.

I paused my work on another book to write this "little project," which turned out to be not so little. I have seen, time and time again, that God gets us to commit at the level that He knows we are capable of. This guide may not seem like much, but maybe God is presenting you a simple opportunity to pray. I wish I could visit every one of your doorsteps like a Baptist deacon and tell you in

ALL CAPS that you can't even comprehend how much God loves you. That if you sat and pondered every single moment of every day, you wouldn't begin to understand how much He longs to speak to *you*. The last thing I would tell you in my church pamphlet would be that no matter what, please don't quit. Every obstacle, disappointment, and doubt is going to come in the hopes that you stop pursuing intimacy with God.

I stood on a platform and told a group, "If you guys knew some of things I've thought or done in my life, you would run me out of this building. But God, knowing every wicked thought and desire, wants to use me anyway." God knows everything about you; you don't have to hide like Adam and Eve. You can stand in confidence before the throne, not because of what you have done, but because of what *He* has done. You are doing better than you think you are. God is longing to hear from you at every sunrise!

God spoke through His Word, He speaks today through His Spirit, and as long as we're alive, there will be a connection for us to speak to Him. I have anticipated a potential next question: "If it's a conversation, then what are we to say to Him? I've gotten past my list of thanks and needs."

As much as I desire to put this in a digestible framework for you, I don't think one exists. I believe He deeply desires your heart and everything in it. He wants to know it all, everything that makes you jump for joy and all of the things that keep you up at night.

One of the biggest things that will hinder conversation with Him is the moment when we don't feel worthy—the time when the truth might be a little too much. Shame always attempts to silence us.

When we get stuck in our own mess, we isolate ourselves, encourage our community less, and often cut off our time with God.

I received a letter from a teenage girl who has having a little bump in the road. She was in high school and had somehow found herself in a treatment center in California. After losing a close friend, abusing alcohol, and attempting to take her own life, she found herself there—with no phone or friends, on a big property in California. She wrote to me occasionally as she had connected with my YouTube videos. We also had a mutual family friend who gave her approval to contact me while in her program. She had reached the end of the wreckage of a few years on her own path. Her parents saw it best to pull her out of her environment and put her in a new one.

I was so excited to receive her first letter and really felt that it was going to be impactful. I had been praying for her for almost a year, knowing many things about her situation, but I had not heard from her directly. If you look at where she was in the natural, most people would have said she was not doing well. When I opened the letter, I read one of the most honest, irreverent, and raw letters I have yet to receive. She talked about her love for Jesus. She also shared her honest opinions about the church (IN ALL CAPS). She mentioned her short season of anger for allowing God to take her childhood friend. She explained why she over-consumed alcohol and got a crazy tattoo. She told me all of the things she was sure of about God and even included some doubts. Last, she told me something that no one else in her life knew, something that had caused her deep pain and was part of the reason she was at the treatment center. At the end of this story, she lightly apologized for being so honest and signed her name.

I took a huge sigh of relief; my thoughts of her being on the right path were confirmed with such a raw and real letter. Someone who the world would say was in a bad place had arrived exactly where she needed to be. She had told the truth in every word. *She let it all out.*

Someone walking in pride and arrogance, continuing in the wrong direction, would never tell the truth as she did. I cried, laughed, and even thanked God for her letter (cuss words and all). It wouldn't pass for a reading in the synagogue but it warmed my heart. For a short moment, I felt what God feels when we truly let it all out in prayer—when we come before Him not with our polished story but as we really are and where we really are. My love and grace for my friend came not from myself, but it flowed in abundance from the Lord. The only reason I saw her this way was because of how He has treated me in my distress. You will find that in prayer, if you're going to do all the talking, at least tell the truth!

Fear and shame are going to cloud your view: "God, are You sure? Can I really say it all?"

"If you hold onto me for dear life," says God, "I'll get you out of any trouble. I'll give you the best of care if you only get to know and trust Me. Call me and I'll answer. I'll be at your side in bad times. I'll rescue you and then throw you a party. I'll give you a long life, a long drink of salvation!" (Psalm 91:14-16).

I was at a prayer event in Dallas last year. A church that is known for a prayer-centered community opens their doors multiple times a day for people to come pray. About an hour into worship and thanking God, the leader of the meeting got on the microphone. He said, "If anyone would like to come share their testimony, please come up now." A small line formed up front. A girl shared her story of moving to Texas and finding healing from panic attacks. A husband shared his story of his wife's healing. A woman had just left her abusive husband and declared her trust in the Lord.

My goodness, it was as if the room opened up. Things felt normal at first, but during the testimonies the suspense and energy continued to rise. These people let it all out; they cast their pearls up on the altar in front of all of us. What we felt in response was a great big hug from the Father! "And they have conquered him by the blood of the Lamb and by the word of their testimony" (Revelation 12:11).

The more honest we are willing to be in our testimony, the more glory goes to God. If we can't be honest with God in prayer, then we are a long way from being able to boldly proclaim in public all that He has done through us. This is not to shame or condemn you but to invite you into the most beautiful thing I have found: communion with a loving and gentle God.

In Dane Ortlund's book *Gentle & Lowly*, he shares how Jesus described His own heart only one time in the Bible: "Take my yoke upon you, and learn from me, for *I am gentle and lowly in heart*, and you will find rest for your souls" (Matthew 11:29).

He said of Himself, "My heart is gentle and lowly." He does not stand above you to condemn or point fingers. He is not in the circle of people talking about you. He is gentle and lowly, it's who He is.

"Jesus does not love like us. We love until we are betrayed. Jesus continued to the cross despite betrayal. We love until we are forsaken. Jesus loved through forsakenness. We love up to a limit. Jesus loves to the end" (Ortlund).

He feels your pain, suffering, and even your insecurities in prayer. I would argue that He is attracted to you even more in your brokenness. God is not asking for a triple windmill dunk, a million followers, or a hole-in-one. He is asking for a humble and honest spirit before Him. David may have broken his fellowship with God at times, but he always returned with a broken spirit. "You do not desire a sacrifice, or I would offer one. You do not want a burnt offering. The sacrifice you desire is a broken spirit. You will not reject a broken and repentant heart, O God"(Psalm 51:16-17).

It is easy to imagine a healthy prayer life when things are good. We can now stand firm with the truth that God is here for us no matter what. If we find ourselves at a low point, He is with us. With His gentle and lowly heart, it could be argued that He's here for us *even more* in our distress. We are open, humble, and willing. We have very little we can give and so much that we need.

> There's no shadow You won't light up
> Mountain You won't climb up
> Coming after me
> There's no wall You won't kick down
> Lie You won't tear down
> Coming after me

As I was writing this book, I took a trip that I was so excited about. God had opened a window for me to have a few days of rest between ministry jobs. I had my manuscript that I carried with me to work on. I was going to have two days with just me and God. I anticipated and expected how amazing it was going to be.

Midway through the trip, I honestly acted in a way that was not in line with an aspiring Christian author (whatever that means). I did not step into that place of rest God had opened for me. It was nothing crazy, but a way of thinking I thought I had conquered crept back up. I spent those days in shame and stuck in my own mind. I didn't write a single word of the book during that trip.

A few days later, I felt a still, small voice say, "Get back up."

I had done just what I've asked you to do in this book. I had prayed, "God, please forgive me. I won't publish the book. I'll never speak again if that's what You want. I'm so sorry."

"Get back up."

"Create in me a clean heart, O God, and renew a right spirit within me" (Psalm 51:10). This verse is proof that we're not to attempt to heal our own hearts. If this is true, it means it is impossible to do it alone. We must, when times are good and when they're bad, boldly approach the throne of grace.

"We must lay before him what is in us;
not what ought to be in us."

—C. S. Lewis

You are doing better
than you think you are.

XX. STEPS

I hope by now we can all take that deep breath and realize that there are going to be times when we all don't feel like praying. There it is—I said it again and I wasn't struck by lightning. God is not surprised that at times our earthly bodies don't feel like doing holy things. He does however honor and encourage every step that we take toward Him.

With the understanding that prayer is simply talking to God, I want to give you practical steps to carry with you. You'll learn the most as you read the Word, pray to God, and spend time in Christian community. But for me, these tips are the best place to continue no matter where you are.

1. Write your prayers.

If you are writing your prayers, you are praying well. For the first 20 years of my life, I would have told you that I'm scatterbrained and can't remember anything. Once a week I'd rattle off a meaningful and profound prayer, but it was unlikely I'd ever pray it again. I would see cool things in the Scriptures but often forget them.

I am intrigued by the Puritans and many others who saw the significance in a single verse of Scripture. To take a day or week at a time and focus on one scripture was unbelievable to me. Could one verse really continue to speak day after day? When it comes to the one-year Bible, one verse a week would definitely have us in the slow lane. Over the next few weeks, I want to give you permission to focus on the quality of your prayers and not the quantity.

I reached a point in life when I was deciding between jobs and potential cities to live in. I was looking at the whole scenario and couldn't get anywhere. I called my pastor and he gave me the most practical advice on prayer I'd ever received. He told me to pray one prayer for the next 21 days.

After sitting on it, I finally came up with a prayer. I said, "God, what do You have for me next?"

At the end of that 21 days, I packed up my apartment, quit my job, and moved cities. Was God pleased with my one simple prayer? It led me to leave everything and follow Him.

Before ever getting a prayer journal or writing down full prayers, I simply bought a pack of notecards. On one notecard I wrote down every person's name who I wanted to pray for. Over the next few months, all I used was that notecard to pray. Something as insignificant as writing on a note card is filled with great power when God is involved.

The final piece to writing your prayers is to keep a journal of your overall time with God. Write down the things you feel or sense as you pray. Some days I'll sit down to listen to music and pray and only write one sentence. It all matters! No matter what you feel, write it down, because you won't remember it later!

2. Speak your prayers.

The devil loves to keep us silent. Just look throughout the history of the Bible: prophets were either speaking or driven to silence.

There's so much power when you decide to pray to God. I love the thought of meditating and praying alone in silence. He honors any way that we pray. There is however something significant about speaking what God has put in your heart. There are moments to enjoy the silence, and there are others when your voice matters. You wouldn't talk to your friend only in your mind. You wouldn't come home to your spouse and not speak to them for the evening.

I will be the first to tell you that speaking your prayers on some days is the last thing you'll want to do. Shame, fear, and discouragement mostly lead us to a place of silence. We often want to be unbothered and alone to sulk in our feelings for a while. There's no problem with sitting in your feelings; in fact, I would encourage it.

Contrary to popular belief, you're allowed to have a bad day as a follower of Jesus. It's okay to say,

"I'm not exactly sure how I got here."
"Why do I feel this way?"
"They're getting on my nerves."
"God, I don't understand what You're doing here."

Admitting your frustration or concern counts as speaking your prayers. You are pushing past the barrier of silence to call out to God. You are sitting in the reality of the moment and inviting God into it. No matter our emotional state, our Father is with us, covering us with mercy and grace.

To speak bold and faith-filled prayers proclaims who God is and sends your doubts packing. It is not going to feel natural. You may not enjoy public speaking or talking, but keep in mind that this is a private place with you and God. You are having a one-on-one coffee date with the Creator of the universe. You're not auditioning for a play or interviewing for a job. Put on your pajamas, make a cup of tea, and be yourself!

3. Remember your prayers.

To remember your prayers is simply to give thanks. As we approach God, bring up our needs, and at times wrestle things out, we have to remember to keep a heart of gratitude.

Business leaders always teach you to decide early on how you're going to measure success. John Maxwell judges success as "those who are closest to me, love and respect me the most." With this choice, he could lose every book deal, crash all of his companies, and give away his money and still go to bed a success.

For me, the foundation of prayer is my relationship with the Father. What He has done for me, how He has treated me, and the way He loves me are incomparable. A heart of gratitude for who He is and what He's done is now the foundation of my prayer life. If every prayer goes unanswered for the next 30 days, I can still wake up with the right attitude: Good morning, Lord. Thank You!

My heart of thankfulness and praise flows outside of my need for things and is rooted in my love for Him.

When you write your prayers, there will be moments when you can look back over them and clearly see where God came through. You took the time to write them down, now you can check off the times when God answered them.

Remembering your prayers and seeing where God came through build up your faith. They also give us a testimony of prayer for others.

You begin to tell others of God's faithfulness and the way He comforted you through trials. You won't have to look far to see the people in your life who only gossip, complain, and live in fear.

By building up your inner prayer life, you give others an example to follow. With your new understanding of prayer, you'll be able to help give them a framework for the troubles they face.

A life of prayer is a call to know Him
more, to sit with Him and invite Him into
all things.

No matter what you're feeling,
invite Him into it.

Pray.

XXI. THE GREAT TEACHER

It took me almost two years to write this book. I studied the topic of prayer for about the same amount of time. I've read the Scriptures, skimmed the commentaries, and rush-ordered the Amazon books. I have spent a great deal of time learning to write and teach on prayer.

But I am not Jesus, the great teacher and example worth following.

I could spend the rest of my life on the topic of prayer and there would still be more to learn. As you continue, I pray that you will draw near to Him, through the power of the Holy Spirit, and let Him teach you. I believe the framework and collections presented will do their part to assist you.

The Father Himself knows you better than I ever could. He will walk with you and show you a custom-tailored plan just for you. Where you're weak, He'll be strong. When you can't see, He'll be your sight.

No matter where you are in life, doubt is going to come. It will try to tell you a story about yourself that is very different than what the Scriptures teach. God speaks to our true identity, that in Him we are holy, flawless, and restored. Because of Jesus, we now stand before Him without a single fault.

My deepest prayer is that you'll begin the work of building your life on the right foundation, that you'll have the conversations with God that will help form you into someone you could have never dreamed of.

Jesus doesn't have a self-help book and He probably never will. There isn't a podcast, YouTube video, or book that is going to truly transform your life like He can.

Becoming like Jesus is our only thing worth pursuing.

Seek first the Kingdom, then you get the rest.

Cultivating a life of talking with God will put you on a foundation that can withstand any storm on the horizon. With all of the divisiveness in our world, there's one thing we can agree on: life is uncertain. We can make our plans, but aside from eternity, we truly don't know what will happen to us. The time to prepare for trouble is not when it arrives.

There will be moments when your prayer life will feel like tilling the ground going uphill, and other days when it will be like riding in a convertible on a cool day. No matter what emotions and feelings come, I can promise you one thing: it's going to be worth it.

If you don't quit. If you continue to walk, talk, and rest with Him.

"I tell you the truth, anyone who believes in me will do the same works I have done, and even greater works, because I am going to be with the Father. You can ask for anything in my name, and I will do it, so that the Son can bring glory to the Father. Yes, ask me for anything in my name, and I will do it!"

John 14:12-14

IT'S GOING
TO BE
WORTH IT